Talking Drums

Talking Drums

ØØØ

An African-American
Quote Collection

COMPILED AND EDITED BY
Anita Doreen Diggs

ST. MARTIN'S GRIFFIN ❧ NEW YORK

Library of Congress Cataloging-in-Publication Data

Talking drums : an African-American quote collection /
    [compiled] by Anita Doreen Diggs.
        p.   cm.
    ISBN 0-312-14138-6
    1. Afro-Americans—Quotations. I. Diggs, Anita Doreen.
PN6081.3.T35   1996
081'.08996—dc20   95-43689
                                                        CIP

First St. Martin's Griffin Edition: February 1996
        10   9   8   7   6   5   4   3   2   1

I am grateful to the following sources for their permission to quote certain of the lengthier selections in this work: Words from *100 Best Colleges for African-American Students* by Erlene B. Wilson. Copyright © 1993 by Erlene B. Wilson. Used by permission of Dutton Signet, a division of Penguin Books USA Inc.

Words from *In The Company of My Sisters* by Julia Boyd. Copyright © 1993 by Julia Boyd. Used by permission of Dutton Signet, a division of Penguin Books USA Inc.

Words from *The Man Behind The Sound Bite: The Real Story of the Rev. Al Sharpton* by Michael Klein, Castillo International, Inc. 1991. Used by Permission.

Words from *The Measure of Our Success* by Marion Wright Edelman. Copyright © 1992 by Marian Wright Edelman. Reprinted by permission of Beacon Press.

Words from *Children of the Dream* by Audrey Edwards and Dr. Craig Polite. Used by permission of Doubleday Books, a division of Bantam Doubleday Dell, Inc.

Words from *Daughters of the Dust* by Julie Dash. Copyright © 1992 by Julie Dash. Reprinted with permission by The New Press.

Words from *Having Our Say* by Sarah and A. Elizabeth Delany with Amy Hill Hearth. Published by Kodansha America Inc. Copyright © by Amy Hill Hearth, Sarah Louise and Annie Elizabeth Delany.

Words from *Black Legacy: America's Hidden Heritage* by William D. Pierson (Amherst: The University of Massachusetts Press, 1993), Copyright © 1993 by The University of Massachusetts Press.

Words from the book *I Dream a World: Portraits of Black Women Who Changed America.* Copyright © 1989 by Brian Lanker. Reprinted by permission of Stewart, Tabori and Chang, Publishers.

Words from *The Heart of a Woman* by Maya Angelou. Reprinted by permission of Random House, Inc.

Words from *Every Goodbye Ain't Gone* by Itabari Njeri. Reprinted by permission of Random House Inc.

Words from *Miles: The Autobiography* by Miles Davis w/Quincy Troupe. Reprinted by permission of Simon & Schuster, Inc.

Words from *Work Sister Work* by Cydney Shields and Leslie C. Shields. Copyright © 1993 by Cydney Shields and Leslie C. Shields. Published by arrangement with Carol Publishing Group. A Birch Lane Press Book.

This book is dedicated to my mother, Mrs. Gladys Haigler-Smith, a wonderful person who is responsible for all of my accomplishments.

∅ Table of Contents ∅

∅ Introduction ∅

Talking Drums is one of the most extensive collections of African-American statements to ever appear in book form. The following chapters contain over six hundred famous and not-so-famous quotations by African-Americans. In making the selections, I chose statements not for their familiarity but for their continuing relevance as we head into the twenty-first century.

The quotations are chronologically arranged according to the year in which the speaker made the statement. Where that is not possible, the quotation is presented according to the copyright or publication date of the source. The chronological order of these quotations helps put them in context and depicts progresson of thought and/or circumstances in the African-American community.

Whenever possible, I've included the source or identification of the quotation hoping to pique the reader's curiosity and stimulate further reading about African-American people, culture, problems, and aspirations. In addition, a Biographical List appears (on p. 159) so that reader may look up unfamiliar names.

Talking Drums reveals the inner thoughts, joy, anger, ambition, and bitter humor of African-Americans from all walks of life. It is a book that can evoke powerful memories of the past and, hopefully, improve the future.

Talking Drums

Ø Ø Ø

⌀ Ability ⌀

"I made the most of my ability and I did my best with my title."
   JOE LOUIS
   1964

"Most whites, even when they credit a Negro with some intelligence, will still feel that all he can talk about is the race issue. . . . Just notice how rarely you will hear whites asking any Negroes what they think about the problem of world health or the space race to land men on the moon."
   MALCOLM X
   1965

"Champions aren't made in gyms. Champions are made from something they have deep inside them—a desire, a dream, a vision. They have to have last-minute stamina, they have to be a little faster, they have to have the skill, and the will. But the will must be stronger than the skill."
   MUHAMMAD ALI
   The Greatest, 1975

"Black minds and talent have skills to control a spacecraft or scalpel with the same finesse and dexterity with which they control a basketball."
   RONALD MCNAIR
   1983

"Helped are those who create anything at all, for they shall relive the thrill of their own conception and realize a partnership in the creation of the Universe that keeps them responsible and cheerful."
   ALICE WALKER
   The Temple of My Familiar, 1989

"I was raised to believe that excellence is the best deterrent to racism or sexism. And that's how I operate my life."

OPRAH WINFREY
I Dream a World, 1989

"I don't doubt what my ability to play baseball has done for me."

HANK AARON
1991

"Excellence is the name of the game no matter what color or what country you're from. If you are the best at what you're doing, then you have my admiration and respect."

JUDITH JAMISON
Black Elegance, February 1994

∅ *Abortion* ∅

"If men could get pregnant, abortion would be a sacrament."
FLORYNCE R. KENNEDY
Ms., March 1973

"I am appalled at the ethical bankruptcy of those who preach a 'right to life' that means, under present social policies, a bare existence in utter misery for many poor women and their children."
SUPREME COURT JUSTICE THURGOOD MARSHALL
1977

"... It is every woman's individual right to make up her own mind about what she is going to do if she faces the question of whether or not she should have an abortion ... it is completely inappropriate for the federal government to inject itself—or for the state government to inject itself—into that situation."
CONGRESSMAN ALAN WHEAT
Speech in Kansas City, Missouri, September 19, 1989

"If we can't preserve the privacy of our right to procreate, I can't imagine what rights we will be able to protect."
FAYE WATTLETON
Time, December 11, 1989

"[Abortion opponents] love little babies as long as they are in somebody else's uterus."
DR. JOYCELYN ELDERS
The New York Times, December 31, 1993

"I am still upset and emotional [since the abortion]. I have had nightmares for over a year about pictures of dead babies."

ROBIN FLANIGAN
The New York Times, January 16, 1994

"My choice was pro-me."

KIMBERLY A. COLLINS
Essence, March 1994

∅ Affirmative Action ∅

"Affirmative action is scarcely a means of mass uplift."

THOMAS SOWELL
The New York Times Magazine, August 8, 1976

"...It must be remembered that during most of the past two hundred years, the Constitution as interpreted by this Court did not prohibit the most ingenious and pervasive forms of discrimination against the Negro. Now, when a State acts to remedy the effects of that legacy of discrimination, I cannot believe that this same Constitution stands as a barrier."

SUPREME COURT JUSTICE THURGOOD MARSHALL
1978

"Affirmative-action programs go beyond racism to create opportunities for those who would otherwise be denied them. Companies with affirmative-action programs hire far more blacks and women and have far more black and women managers than other companies."

JOHN E. JACOB
Speech in New Orleans, July 31, 1983

"I am strained to defend racial quotas and any affirmative action that supersedes merit. And I believe there was much that Reagan had to offer blacks."

SHELBY STEELE
The Content of Our Character, 1990

"White Anglo-Saxon males never have felt inferior as a result of their centuries of 'affirmative action' and quotas ... in jobs from which Jews, racial minorities, and women were excluded and too often still are."

MARIAN WRIGHT EDELMAN
The Measure of Our Success, 1992

"Practically, affirmative action is probably necessary. But I would not want to know that I received a job simply because I am black. Affirmative action tends to undermine the spirit of individual initiative."

ARTHUR ASHE
Days of Grace, 1992

"What amazes me is the naiveté of my white friends who believe that affirmative action and quotas have removed barriers for blacks."

LOBBYIST
Work Sister Work, 1993

"If stereotyping, double standards and professional ceilings exist quite independently of formal racial-preference programs, how eager should we be to join the movement to abolish affirmative action?"

ELLIS COSE
The Rage of a Privileged Class, 1993

"White women have benefited the most from affirmative action."

ANITA DOREEN DIGGS
Success at Work: A Guide for African-Americans, 1993

"In the booming affirmative action years, from 1973 to 1982 . . . companies devised programs to *hire* us but not to *keep* us or help us develop skills. When affirmative action ended, many of us were out of work because we weren't seen as valuable players."

ANDREA DAVIS PINKNEY
Essence, March 1994

∅ America ∅

"... America is as much our country, as it is yours."
DAVID WALKER
Walker's Appeal, September 28, 1829

"Go where you may, search where you will, roam through all the monarchies and despotisms of the Old World, travel through South America, search out every abuse, and when you have found the last, lay your facts by the side of the every-day practices of this nation, and you will say with me that, for revolting barbarity and shameless hypocrisy, America reigns without a rival...."
FREDERICK DOUGLASS
Speech in Rochester, New York, 1852

"Men talk of the Negro problem; there is no Negro problem. The problem is whether American people have loyalty enough, honor enough, patriotism enough, to live up to their own constitution."
PAUL LAURENCE DUNBAR
August 25, 1893

"Would America have been America without her Negro people?"
W. E. B. DuBois
The Souls of Black Folk, 1903

"The position of the Negro in American culture is indeed a paradox. It almost passes understanding how and why a group of people can be socially despised, yet at the same time artistically esteemed and culturally influential."
ALAIN LOCKE
The Negro in American Culture, 1929

"Wese a mingled people."

> ZORA NEALE HURSTON
> *Jonah's Gourd Vine, 1934*

"I am born and bred in this America of ours. I want to love
it. I love part of it. But it's up to the rest of America when I
shall love it with the same intensity that I love the Negro
people from whom I sprang."

> PAUL ROBESON
> 1947

"America is woven of many strands; I would recognize them
and let it so remain.... Our fate is to become one, and yet
many. This is not prophecy, but description."

> RALPH ELLISON
> *Invisible Man,* 1952

"Despite the terrorization which the Negro in America endured and endures sporadically until today, despite the cruel
and totally inescapable ambivalence of his status in this country, the battle for his identity has long ago been won. He is
not a visitor to the West, but a citizen there, an American."

> JAMES BALDWIN
> *Notes of a Native Son,* 1955

"I am not anti-American. I think there are plenty of good
people in America, but there are also plenty of bad people in
America—and the bad ones are the ones that seem to have
all the power."

> MALCOLM X
> 1964

"To be a Negro in America is to hope against hope."

> MARTIN LUTHER KING, JR.
> *Where Do We Go from Here: Chaos or Community?,* 1967

"America will tolerate the taking of human life without giving it a second thought. But don't misuse a household pet."

DICK GREGORY
The Shadow that Scares Me, 1968

"I hear that melting-pot stuff a lot, and all I can say is that we haven't melted."

JESSE JACKSON
Playboy, November 1969

"We really are fifteen countries and it's really remarkable that each of us thinks we represent the real America. The Midwesterner in Kansas, the black American in Durham—both are certain they are the real American."

MAYA ANGELOU
Time, April 24, 1978

"I am proud to be a black American."

MICHAEL JACKSON
Time, February 22, 1993

"I would like to see reparations, redressings, and repatriation for African-Americans in New York and across this country. America owes us for the atrocities and the damage they have done. . . ."

QUEEN MOTHER MOORE
The Daily News, February 27, 1994

∅ Ancestry ∅

"I teach the kings of their ancestors so that the lives of the
ancients might serve them as an example, for the world is old
but the future springs from the past."

MAMADOU KOUYATE
Sundiata: An Epic of Old Mali, 1217–1237A.D.

"In Garvey's time the 'Back to Africa' movement had an appeal
and probably made some sense. But it doesn't make any sense
now . . . because the black people of America aren't Africans
anymore, and the Africans don't want them. . . ."

CHESTER HIMES
1964

"Many people will teach you that the Black man in this country
doesn't identify with Africa. Before 1959, many Negroes didn't.
But before 1959, the image of Africa was created by an enemy
of Africa, because Africans weren't in a position to create and
project their own images. Such an image of the Africans was
so hateful to Afro-Americans that they refused to identify with
Africa. We did not realize that in hating Africa and the Africans
we were hating ourselves. You cannot hate the roots of a tree
and not hate the tree itself."

MALCOLM X
Speech at Harvard University, December 16, 1964

"I had a heritage, rich and nearer than the tongue which gave
it voice. My mind resounded with the words and my blood
raced to the rhythms."

MAYA ANGELOU
The Heart of a Woman, 1981

"All of us [blacks worldwide] are bound to Mother Africa by invisible but tenacious bonds. . . ."

ARCHBISHOP DESMOND TUTU
The Words of Desmond Tutu, 1984

"The loss of our African culture is a tragic fact of history, and the conflict it poses is a profound one that has divided blacks many times since Emancipation: Do we accept the loss and assimilate totally or do we try to reclaim our culture and synthesize it with our present reality?"

ITABERI NJERI
Every Good-bye Ain't Gone, 1990

"I am very much aware of my black heritage, but I'm also aware of the other elements of who I am. And I think sometimes it bothers people [who want me to say] that I'm black and that's it. . . . When people ask, I say I'm black, Venezuelan, and Irish because that's who I am."

MARIAH CAREY
Ebony, April 1994

∅ Arts ∅

"The Negro artist works against an undertow of sharp criticism and misunderstanding from his own group and unintentional bribes from the whites. . . . 'O, be respectable, write about nice people, show how good we are' say the Negroes. . . . 'Be stereotyped, don't go too far, don't shatter our illusions about you, don't amuse us too seriously. We will pay you,' say the whites."

    LANGSTON HUGHES
    The Nation, June 23, 1926

"Most of our shows are financed, staged, and directed by white men and most of these white men arrogate the right to tell us when and how. . . ."

    SALEM TUTT-WHITNEY
    Chicago Defender, November 1, 1930

"Certainly Hollywood has been making films lately starring black actors, but the blackness of the character is always the cause of the conflict in the story. Writers and producers seem to think that you need a special reason for a role to be played by a Negro. . . ."

    BILL COSBY
    Jet, October 1967

"The reason I became ballerina of the Metropolitan Opera was because I couldn't be topped. You don't get there *because,* you get there *in spite of.*"

    JANET COLLINS
    I Dream a World, 1989

"The trailer for *Boyz 'N the Hood* made it look like a gang movie and it wasn't. Who produced the trailer that was shown on the TV?"

LUTHER CAMPBELL
As Nasty as They Wanna Be, 1992

"I'm tired of *Miss Daisy* ... I am tired of books and movies and plays written by white folks about the good old days when servants were patient, loyal, long-suffering, and black."

PEARL CLEAGE
Deals with the Devil and Other Reasons to Riot, 1993

". . . It is important for African-American writers and directors to develop projects with better characters, so they can have an impact on the images that are being shown."

STEVE SANFORD
Black Elegance, February 1994

"There are lots of strong African-American women like her [Valaida Snow], Rosa Parks, and Fannie Lou Hamer whose stories need to be told."

ELLA JOYCE
Black Elegance, February 1994

"There is not one black person who can 'green light' a television project, who can say 'yes, let's make that film or put that show on the air. . . .' "

TIM REID
Essence, March 1994

"I'm told he [Norman Lear] turned over every stone looking for every African-American actor on the continent before he finally decided to talk to me about the show. When we got together for *704 Hauser,* he told me frankly that he was concerned how we would get along. . . ."

JOHN AMOS
The Daily News/New York Vue, March 13–19, 1994

∅ Athletes ∅

"I'm not a Negro tennis player. I'm a tennis player."
ALTHEA GIBSON
1959

"Will somebody please tell me what Althea Gibson is if she is not a Negro tennis player? Did the Negroes who housed, fed, clothed, and educated her, free of charge, do so because she was a tennis player or because she is a Negro tennis player? Did the American Tennis Association fight for her to get a chance to play in the big national tournaments because she was a tennis player or because she is a Negro tennis player?"
P. L. PRATTIS
Pittsburgh Courier, August 8, 1959

"Where do you think I would be next week if I didn't know how to shout and holler and make the public sit up and take notice? I would be poor, for one thing, and I would probably be down in Louisville, Kentucky (my home town), washing windows or running an elevator an' saying 'yes suh' and 'no suh' and knowing my place. Instead of that, I'm saying I'm one of the highest paid athletes in the world . . . and that I'm the greatest fighter in the world. . . ."
CASSIUS CLAY
Sports Illustrated, February 24, 1964

"I hated the sight on TV of big, clumsy, lumbering heavy-weights plodding, stalking each other like two Frankenstein monsters, clinging, slugging toe to toe. I knew I could do it better. I would be as fast as a lightweight, circle, dance, shuffle, hit, and move . . . dance again and make an art out of it."
MUHAMMAD ALI
The Greatest, 1975

"...The black athlete carries the image of the black community. He carries the cross, in a way, until blacks make inroads in other dimensions."

ARTHUR ASHE
The New York Times, October 26, 1982

"Ask any athlete: We all hurt at times. I'm asking my body to go through seven different tasks. To ask it not to ache would be too much."

JACKIE JOYNER-KERSEE
Time, September 19, 1988

"When I'm playing, I'm relaxed. . . . I'm like a fish in water."

BO JACKSON
Time, April 1, 1991

"When people start talking about baseball players not deserving the money they are getting paid, I tell them to mind their own business . . . I don't care what people say, I'm worth it."

BARRY BONDS
Ebony, September 1993

"I definitely believe this is my greatest triumph. . . . What I learned was the heptathlon is a test of strength and character and of my heart."

JACKIE JOYNER-KERSEE
Jet, September 6, 1993

"In many ways he [Anfernee Hardaway] reminds me of myself when I was much younger. So many guys have been compared to me and they all flop. But Anfernee is the first guy that really is like me."

EARVIN "MAGIC" JOHNSON
The Daily News, February 27, 1994

∅ Business ∅

"You know why Madison Avenue advertising has never done well in Harlem? We're the only ones who know what it means to be brand X."

DICK GREGORY
From the Back of the Bus, 1962

"When it comes to banking, Negroes want secrecy. They don't want the rest of Harlem to know what they're doing, what money they're making, how big their deposits are."

GUICHARD PARRIS
Certain People: America's Black Elite, 1977

"As early as 1901, West Indians owned 20 percent of all black businesses in Manhattan, although they were only 10 percent of the black population there."

THOMAS SOWELL
Ethnic America, 1981

"A lot of people gave themselves bad advice. There are at least two people who would be multimillionaires today if they had invested the $1,000 I was asking for forty-seven years ago."

JOHN H. JOHNSON
Succeeding Against the Odds, 1989

"Spike Lee accused Eddie [Murphy]. He said any man who makes a billion dollars should demand more black participation at Paramount. Standing on the outside doing *She's Gotta Have It*, you don't understand the big leagues. If Eddie went in and told [Paramount Chairman] Frank Mancuso to do something, he'd tell Eddie to fuck off."

ARSENIO HALL
Ebony, May 1990

"I plan to be a major player in the entertainment industry. It's about time there was a black man who doesn't have to give up his blackness in order to play with the white guys."

RUSSELL SIMMONS
Black Enterprise, December 1992

"I'm setting up trust funds for [my sons] to go to the best colleges my money can pay for. I would rather see them as young, smart, black businessmen than as athletes because everybody knows what a black athlete is."

BO JACKSON
Jet, August 2, 1993

"I don't want to do anything to negatively affect a young kid regardless of how hard the [rap] label wants me to be or what the market will bear for me to be ... if that's gonna cost me some sales, then fine."

YOUNG M.C.
Black Beat, October 1993

"There is no problem with commercializing it [Kwanzaa], but who will be the benefactors of the commercialization? It should be people of African descent, not just corporate America."

CEDRIC MCCLESTER, Spokesman Kwanzaa Holiday Expo 1993
The New York Times, December 20, 1993

"We need to run our own businesses more, and we need to run them the way DuBois ran Niagara, the way Healy ran Georgetown, the way Johnson ran *Jet*, the way Gaston ran part of Birmingham, the way Gordy ran Motown, the way Reggie Lewis ran Beatrice."

RALPH WILEY
What Black People Should Do Now, 1993

"The white girls I know get offered $1 million or $1 million 5, and they [Cover Girl Cosmetics] offered me $100,000."

KAREN ALEXANDER
The Daily News, February 27, 1994

"... If we [women] could go to banks and get a [business] loan, the whole face of Harlem could change...."

DOROTHY PITMAN HUGHES
The New York Times, February 27, 1994

"I think he [Ken Hamblin] is a jerk ... I couldn't get a job for years in general-market radio.... The reason this guy's got a job is because of the dues paid by people like me...."

ED CASTLEBERRY
The Daily News, February 27, 1994

"Before I got signed, I read anything I could about the music business—especially about the Motown days when people sold millions of singles and saw no money.... So I made a point to know what was going on with me contractually."

TONI BRAXTON
Essence, April 1994

∅ *Character* ∅

"A man's character always takes its hue, more or less, from the form and color of things about him."

FREDERICK DOUGLASS
Life and Times of Frederick Douglass, 1892

"...None of us is responsible for the complexion of his skin...this fact of nature offers no clue to the character or quality of the person underneath."

MARIAN ANDERSON
1941

"A man who tosses worms in the river isn't necessarily a friend to the fish."

MALCOLM X
June 1963

"When a man does something or possesses something that is complementary to his character, it is virtually impossible for him to hide this thing [or] keep it to himself."

GEORGE JACKSON
Soledad Brother: The Prison Letters of George Jackson, 1964

"There's a period of life when we swallow a knowledge of ourselves and it becomes either good or sour inside."

PEARL BAILEY
The Raw Pearl, 1968

"The need for change bulldozed a road down the center of my mind."

MAYA ANGELOU
I Know Why the Caged Bird Sings, 1970

"A man without ambition is dead. A man with ambition but no love is dead. A man with ambition and love for his blessings here on earth is ever so alive."

PEARL BAILEY
Talking to Myself, 1971

"A word to the wise ain't necessary—it's the stupid ones who need advice."

BILL COSBY
Fat Albert's Survival Kit, 1975

"We must change in order to survive."

PEARL BAILEY
Hurry Up American and Split, 1976

"Misplaced emphasis occurs . . . when you think that everything is going well because your car drives so smoothly and your new suit fits you so well, and those high-priced shoes you bought make your feet feel so good; and you begin to believe that these things, these many luxuries all around, are the really important matters of your life."

MARTIN LUTHER KING, SR.
Daddy King, 1980

"I make bold to assert that it took more courage for Martin Luther King, Jr. to practice nonviolence than it took his assassin to fire the fatal shot."

DR. BENJAMIN E. MAYS
Quotable Quotes of Benjamin Mays, 1984

"If Rosa Parks had not refused to move to the back of the bus, you and I might never have heard of Dr. Martin Luther King."

RAMSEY CLARK
The New York Times, April 14, 1987

"It takes a whole lot of courage to come out in blackface in front of 3,000 people. I don't care if you don't like it. I do."

WHOOPI GOLDBERG
The Daily News, October 9, 1993

"In every issue we feature African-Americans who, by taking full responsibility for their lives, have not only survived adversity but prevailed. . . . Difficult is no longer a word I accept."

SUSAN TAYLOR
The Daily News, January 30, 1994

"There will always be some curve balls in your life. Teach your children to thrive in that adversity."

JEANNE MOUTOUSSAMY-ASHE
Working Woman, April 1994

"We need quiet time to examine our lives openly and honestly . . . spending quiet time alone gives your mind an opportunity to renew itself and create order."

SUSAN TAYLOR
Essence, March 1994

∅ Childhood ∅

"Summer. Bright hot days. Hunger still a vital part of my consciousness . . . Loneliness . . . Reading . . . Doubt . . . Fear . . . This was my reality in 1924."

RICHARD WRIGHT
Black Boy, 1937

"I never had a chance to play with dolls like other kids. I started working when I was six years old."

BILLIE HOLIDAY
1948

"Evenings were spent mainly on the back porches where screen doors slammed in the darkness with those really very special summertime sounds. And, sometimes, when Chicago nights got too steamy, the whole family got into the car and went to the park and slept out in the open on blankets."

LORRAINE HANSBERRY
To Be Young, Gifted and Black, 1960

". . . As anti-white as my father was, he was subconsciously so afflicted with the white man's brainwashing of Negroes that he inclined to favor the light ones and I was his lightest child."

MALCOLM X
The Autobiography of Malcolm X, 1965

"At fifteen, life had taught me undeniably that surrender, in its place, was as honorable as resistance, especially if one had no choice."

MAYA ANGELOU
I Know Why the Caged Bird Sings, 1970

"During childhood I wasn't aware that there was segregation. . . . White people just seemed very alien and strange to me."

ALICE WALKER
I Dream a World, 1989

"The essence of childhood, of course, is play, which my friends and I did endlessly on streets that we reluctantly shared with traffic."

BILL COSBY
Childhood, 1991

"After school, I could never run off and play like the other kids. I had to go to dance—tap, ballet and African—or acting classes. . . . I hated it back then, but now I am grateful for that foundation."

THERESA RANDLE
Essence, April 1994

"Home in Gary was a small, plainly furnished one-story house. . . . It was simple and nondescript, but we . . . never felt that we were poor or in any way deprived."

LATOYA JACKSON
LaToya: Growing Up in the Jackson Family, 1991

"We lived in a number of raggedy houses. The basement of our house was always flooded and I remember we used to have to get in this little boat my brother had gotten for Christmas and paddle over to the washer and dryer to get the clothes in and out."

TERRY MCMILLAN
Ebony, May 1993

". . . I really enjoyed my childhood. . . ."

DIANA ROSS
Secrets of a Sparrow, 1993

∅ Children ∅

"I looked at that kid for a long time, I felt something impossible for me to explain in words. Then when they took [Natalie] away, it hit me. I got scared all over again and began to feel giddy. Then it came to me. I was a father."

NAT "KING" COLE
Unforgettable: The Mystique of Nat "King" Cole, 1950

"The sins of the fathers are visited upon the heads of their children—but only if the children continue in the evil deeds of the fathers."

ELDRIDGE CLEAVER
Soul on Ice, 1968

"Children's talent to endure stems from their ignorance of alternatives."

MAYA ANGELOU
I Know Why the Caged Bird Sings, 1970

"Just because a child's parents are poor or uneducated is no reason to deprive the child of basic human rights to health care, education, proper nutrition. Clearly we ignore the needs of black children, poor children, and handicapped children in this country."

MARIAN WRIGHT EDELMAN
Psychology Today, June 1975

"Children are a wonderful gift. . . . They have an extraordinary capacity to see into the heart of things and to expose sham and humbug for what they are."

ARCHBISHOP DESMOND TUTU
The Words of Desmond Tutu, 1984

"Two parents can't raise a child any more than one. You need a whole community—everybody—to raise a child. . . ."

TONI MORRISON
Time, May 22, 1989

"A white child might need a role model, but a black child needs more than that in this society. He needs hope."

HANK AARON
I Had a Hammer, 1991

"I think children are a mirror reflection of their parents. If I don't curse, steal, lie, cheat, and disrespect people, they will pick up on that."

EARL OFARI HUTCHINSON, PH.D.
Black Fatherhood: The Guide To Male Parenting, 1992

". . . Most boys who grow up in fatherless homes do *not* become homosexual. At the same time, many homosexuals grew up in homes where fathers were present. The reasons for homosexuality are complex and depend on a variety of biological and environmental factors."

JAMES P. COMER, M.D. and ALVIN F. POUSSAINT, M.D.
Raising Black Children, 1992

"I think the ideal situation is to have a mom and a pop raising the child. I wouldn't tell people the best way to raise a child is in a single-parent household."

SPEECH
Essence, November 1993

"I'm too selfish right now with my career to have children."

HALLE BERRY
National Enquirer, February 8, 1994

Ø Christmas Ø

"The only respite from the constant labor the slave has through the whole year is during the Christmas holidays. . . . It is the time of feasting, and frolicking, and fiddling—the carnival season with the children of bondage."

SOLOMON NORTHUP
Twelve Years a Slave, 1853

"All the Christmas we had was Old Master would kill a hog and give us a piece of pork. We thought that was something, and the way Christmas lasted was 'cording to the big sweet-gum backlog. When that burned out, the Christmas was over."

BOOKER T. WASHINGTON
Up from Slavery, 1900

"There'd been a couple of Christmases when it seemed like there was no way we'd have meat, but somehow my momma always made that kind of miracle happen and there it was, on the table, when you woke up Christmas morning."

JESSE OWENS
Jesse Owens: The Man Who Outran Hitler, 1978

"When I first told my wife I was thinking about observing Kwanzaa, she barred the way to our attic and said she'd never chuck our Christmas tree lights and antique ornaments. I told her that wouldn't be necessary. Kwanzaa . . . does not replace Christmas and is not a religious holiday. It is a time to focus on Africa and African-inspired culture and to reinforce a value system that goes back for generations."

ERIC V. COPAGE
Kwanzaa: An African-American Celebration of Cooking and Culture, 1991

"After touring most of the year, I look forward to being home for the holidays!"

WHITNEY HOUSTON
Ebony, December 1993

"The challenge for the African people is to avoid the problems of commercialization that they've learned from other holidays like Christmas."

DR. MAULANA KARENGA, Creator of Kwanzaa
The New York Times, December 20, 1993

"For the first time, there will be no gift-giving—at least gifts that come from a store. The gifts we exchange this year will be expressions of love and appreciation that come from the heart."

HALLE BERRY
Ebony, December 1993

∅ Civil Rights ∅

"Once our freedom struggle is lifted from the confining civil-rights label to the level of human rights, our struggle then becomes internationalized."

MALCOLM X
1964

"When somebody asks us 'What do you want?' We should answer 'What have *you* got?'"

REVEREND JAMES BEVEL
1965

"What black folks are given in the U. S. on the installment plan, as in civil-rights bills. Not to be confused with human rights, which are the dignity, stature, humanity, respect, and freedom belonging to all people by right of birth."

DICK GREGORY
Dick Gregory's Political Primer, 1972

"Black people cannot and will not become integrated into American society on any terms but those of self-determination and autonomy."

GERDA LERNER
Black Women in White America, 1972

"Civil Rights is a term that did not evolve out of black culture, but rather, out of American law. As such, it is a term of limitation."

ALICE WALKER
In Search of Our Mother's Gardens, 1983

"Reagan has done zero for civil rights."

SUPREME COURT JUSTICE THURGOOD MARSHALL
1987

∅ *Class* ∅

"However laudable an ambition to rise may be, the first duty of an upper class is to serve the lower classes. The aristocracies of all peoples have been slow in learning this, and perhaps the Negro is no slower than the rest, but his peculiar situation demands that in his case this lesson be learned sooner."

W. E. B. DuBois
The Philadelphia Negro, 1899

"The majority of this [black bourgeoisie] class go through life denouncing white people because they are trying to run away from blacks and decrying the blacks because they are not white."

Carter G. Woodson, Ph.D.
Baltimore Afro-American, January 23, 1932

"The Negro upper class has its present status primarily because of its position in a segregated social world. If members of the Negro upper class were integrated into American society, their occupations and incomes would place them in the middle class."

E. Franklin Frazier
The Negro in the United States, 1957

"I suppose that regardless of what any Negro in America might do or how high he might rise in social status, he still has something in common with every other Negro."

Claude Brown
Manchild in the Promised Land, 1965

"It is not difficult to understand why the black bourgeoisie should seek privacy and each other's company. But if there was ever a time when the black masses—bereft of leadership, dulled by dope, by unemployment, by an official national policy of disregard and disrespect—needed the talented bourgeoisie with their degrees and their expertise, it is now."

ORDE COOMBS
Do You See My Love for You Growing, 1970

"... Someone who dresses in a dashiki and accidentally brushes past a little old white lady may ... be called ... 'damn Black militant' as he hurries to his $25,000 a year job in a white public relations firm."

INEZ SMITH REID
Together Black Woman, 1975

"Black Americans ... do not have a national bourgeoisie with wealth and political power comparable to the Fords, Rockefellers, Mellons, Vanderbilts, Carnegies, or DuPonts. ... In the absence of the correlative power, wealth, and class standing of the white conservative establishment, what, then, is a black conservative and what do blacks have to conserve?"

ROBERT CHRISMAN
Court of Appeal, 1992

"People don't stop being angry just because they get money or get position. ... If you're black and middle class ... everyday you're [going to get] a lot of crap. ..."

Dr. ALVIN POUSSAINT
The Rage of a Privileged Class, 1993

"If [journalist] Pete Hamill thinks it's a good idea for black middle-class people to return to the ghettoes to aid their underclass brothers and sisters, then why isn't it a good idea for

Mr. Hamill to relocate to South Boston or The Bronx to aid the Irish-American underclass?"

ISHMAEL REED
Airing Dirty Laundry, 1994

"Denzel [Washington] isn't just Hollywood hold-your-breath handsome . . . he's polish, culture, class."

ALEXIS HERMAN
Ebony, March 1994

∅ College ∅

"The function of the university is not simply to teach bread-winning or to furnish teachers for the public schools or to be a center of polite society; it is, above all, to be the organ of that fine adjustment between real life and the growing knowledge of life, an adjustment which forms the secret of civilization."

W. E. B. DuBois
The Souls of Black Folk, 1903

"[The leading Negro colleges] do not teach Negroes who they are, what they have done, and what they have to do."

CARTER G. WOODSON, Ph.D.
1931

"In my opinion, Harvard has ruined more Negroes than bad whiskey."

CARTER G. WOODSON, Ph.D.
1933

"Historically, uneven state funding has choked the ability of black colleges and universities to become partners in the mainstream of higher education."

DR. N. JOYCE PAYNE
Jet, November 30, 1992

"College pays and is a fine investment. It doubles your chance of getting a job over a high school graduate. But don't think you can park there or relegate your mind's and soul's growth to what you have learned or will learn at school. Read. Not just what you have to read for class or work, but to learn from the wisdom and joys and mistakes of others."

MARIAN WRIGHT EDELMAN
The Measure of Our Success, 1992

"African-American students on predominantly white college campuses are challenged in ways that other students do not experience. Besides being intellectually ready to achieve academic excellence, African-American students at these schools must be self-confident, self-aware, ambitious, and driven by the mind-set of a crusader on a mission."

ERLENE B. WILSON
The 100 Best Colleges for African-American Students, 1993

Ø

∅ Crime ∅

"Our crime rate is the highest. Negroes fill the jails. The answer, which you will not at the moment comprehend, is $$$$$ dollars."

LANGSTON HUGHES
New York Post, May 21, 1965

". . . Black on black crime has reached a critical level that threatens our existence as a people. It is a threat to our youths, to our women, to our senior citizens, to our institutions, to our values. And although we are not responsible for the external factors that systematically create breeding grounds for social disorder, we cannot avoid the internal responsibility of doing everything we can to solve a problem that is rending the fabric of our lives."

JOHN H. JOHNSON
Ebony, August 1979

"I am absolutely opposed to the death penalty."

Dr. JOYCELYN ELDERS
The New York Times Magazine, January 30, 1994

"Murder is part of the American motif."

SAPPHIRE
The Daily News, February 27, 1994

"Sometimes I would just inflict pain because I thought it gave me power. A lot of the young guys coming up here now still talk the same way, about who they shot and Nines and Uzis. We try to talk to young brothers about stopping this."

RICHARD JACKSON
The Daily News, March 13, 1994

∅ Culture ∅

"The observance of abstinence at the parties of the higher classes of colored society—total abstinence from all that has a tendency to intoxicate—is worthy of remark. So far as my observation has extended, the only drinks that are presented . . . may consist of lemonade, or some pleasant and wholesome syrup commingled with water. No wines of any description—not even the lightest and mildest—are ever brought forward."

> EDITOR
> *Sketches of Higher Classes of Colored Society,* 1841

"Please stop using the word Negro. . . . We are the only human beings in the world with fifty-seven varieties of complexions who are classed together as a single racial unit. Therefore, we are really colored people and that is the only name in the English language which accurately describes us."

> MARY CHURCH TERRELL
> *The Washington Post,* May 14, 1949

"We're a great heart people."

> PEARL BAILEY
> *New York Post,* April 27, 1965

"It isn't a matter of black is beautiful as much as it is white is not *all* that's beautiful."

> BILL COSBY
> *Playboy,* May 1969

"The Office Tom is easy to recognize. If you notice a cocoa-colored person leaping into the air at the slightest hint of white approval, or wiping away tears of mirth when one of the whites on staff tells even a tiny joke, that is probably the Tom."

ANITA DOREEN DIGGS
Success at Work: A Guide for African-Americans, 1993

"This may be 1994, but there is still a plantation mentality at work here. The closer we get to white folks in looks, the more privilege, the more status, the more stature that comes with that. We have that inherently working in our subconsciousness."

MONICA WALKER
The Daily News, February 13, 1994

"Black people don't all have the same experience."

JOHN AMOS
USA Weekend, February 25–27, 1994

"This idea of identity through genetic accident and ethnic costumes dominated by Kente cloth motifs is both misbegotten and fruitless."

STANLEY CROUCH
The Daily News, March 27, 1994

Ø Death Ø

"Death . . . the irreverent disrespector of persons, sparing neither maid nor matron, celebrity nor nonentity. . . ."

COUNTEE CULLEN
1927

"A man who won't die for something is not fit to live."

MARTIN LUTHER KING, JR.
1963

"I know that I could suddenly die at the hands of some white racists . . . or it could be some brainwashed Negro. . . . When I *am* dead, the white man in his press is going to identify me with 'hate.' He will make use of me dead as he has made use of me alive. . . ."

MALCOLM X
The Autobiography of Malcolm X, 1965

". . . A man must be willing to die for justice. Death is an inescapable reality and men die daily, but good deeds live forever."

REVEREND JESSE JACKSON
Jesse Jackson: The Man, The Movement, The Myth, 1975

"It's a blessing to die for a cause, because you can so easily die for nothing."

ANDREW YOUNG
Playboy, July 1977

"If I die tomorrow, I ain't got no regrets."

SAMMY DAVIS, JR.
Jet, 1990

"If you're gonna die, at least be well defined in what you were doing that made it worthwhile."

REVEREND AL SHARPTON
The Daily News, February 13, 1994

"A look at death can change you."

ANFERNEE HARDAWAY
The Daily News, February 27, 1994

"Each year . . . 40,000 to 60,000 African-Americans die from tobacco-related diseases. Many of these deaths are preventable."

DR. LONNIE BRISTOW, President of the American Medical Association
Ebony, March 1994

∅ Democracy ∅

"The American Negro believes in democracy. We want to make it real, complete, workable, not only for ourselves—the thirteen million dark ones—but for all Americans all over the land."

LANGSTON HUGHES
Journal of Educational Sociology, February 1943

"Friends, we are glad to have made you happy. We hope you have enjoyed us. This is the last time I shall play Louisville [Kentucky] because the management refuses to let people like us sit by people like you. Maybe after the war we shall have democracy and I can return."

KATHERINE DUNHAM
1944

"It is ironic that America, supposedly the cradle of democracy, is forced to send the first two Negroes in baseball to Canada in order for them to be accepted."

EDITORIAL
Chicago Defender, April 13, 1946

"This is a great day [decision in Brown v. Board of Education] for the Negro. This is democracy's finest hour."

CONGRESSMAN ADAM CLAYTON POWELL, Jr.
1954

"... Marauding cowboys, outlaws, Prohibition gangsters, klansmen, crack gangs—all corrupt and threaten the meaning of our democracy."

STANLEY CROUCH
The Daily News, April 10, 1994

∅ Dreams ∅

"I have a dream that one day even the state of Mississippi, a desert state sweltering with the heat of injustice and oppression, will be transformed into an oasis of freedom and justice. . . ."

MARTIN LUTHER KING, Jr.
August 28, 1963

"When I used to live in the Brewster Projects, I always thought it would be fantastic to have a phone . . . I would dream about a phone. . . ."

FLORENCE BALLARD
Look, May 1966

"Poor people are allowed the same dreams as everyone else."

KIMI GRAY
Time, December 12, 1988

"I didn't dream about fame. I dreamed about getting my kid more than one pair of shoes, or how to make $165 worth of groceries last all month."

WHOOPI GOLDBERG
Ebony, March 1991

"I never dreamed of filmmaking when I was little. At that time I wanted to be in the secretarial pool, typing away and having fun like the women I saw on TV and in the movies."

JULIE DASH
Daughters of the Dust, 1992

"My life has turned out beyond my wildest dreams. . . . I never could have predicted what has happened to me."

BERTICE BERRY
Essence, April 1994

∅ Drugs ∅

"Dope never helped anybody sing better or play music better or do anything better. All dope can do for you is kill you—and kill you the long, slow, hard way."

BILLIE HOLIDAY
1956

"I don't cope with drugs and don't deal with people who are around them."

KIM FIELDS
Jet, July 15, 1985

"I don't think a person has to use drugs [to excel in athletics]. There is no substitute for hard work."

FLORENCE GRIFFITH JOYNER
Time, September 19, 1988

"I have always thought that narcotics should be legalized so that it wouldn't be that much of a street problem."

MILES DAVIS
Miles: The Autobiography, 1989

"When mayors of great cities are indicted for drug abuse, it should show the depth of the problem."

CONGRESSMAN CHARLES RANGEL (D-NY)
January 1990

"When I was a judge of Recorders Court in Detroit for twelve years, I saw hundreds of men and women come before me charged with drugs.... The criminals were mostly poor, mostly black.... In most cases their privacy had been invaded by an illegal stop, search, and seizure.... If drug use were mostly a white, middle-class problem, addicts would be in treatment centers and hospitals instead of jail...."

CONGRESSMAN GEORGE CROCKETT
Detroit News, February 11, 1990

"Junkies never know they have to stop and I don't know now how I did. I'm the living legacy of this group of talented, wonderful dope fiends who cleaned me up and made a lasting impression."

WHOOPI GOLDBERG
Ebony, March 1991

"I don't support the legalization of drugs. But... should we study the issue, should we consider whether decriminalization makes sense? Consider alternative ways of approaching the issue?... Absolutely."

SENATOR CAROLE MOSELEY-BRAUN (D-IL)
USA Weekend, March 11–13, 1994

"The war on drugs has become a war on the minority community."

REVEREND LEONARD B. JACKSON
USA Weekend, April 8–10, 1994

∅ Economics ∅

"An Italian comes over here from his country to repair shoes in a community of Negroes, and the Greeks to feed them, the Chinese to wash their clothes, and the Jew to sell their merchandise. . . . If we permit foreigners to impoverish us by establishing and controlling businesses [in the black community] which we support, then we ought to starve."

CARTER G. WOODSON, PH.D.
New York Age, January 11, 1936

"The depression brought everybody down a peg or two. And the Negroes had but a few pegs to fall."

LANGSTON HUGHES
The Big Sea, 1940

"You gotta realize, my people have never known what job security is. For instance, come another recession and the economy has to tighten its belt—who do you think's gonna be the first notch?"

DICK GREGORY
From the Back of the Bus, 1962

"Let me tell you what we mean by *economic reciprocity* . . . corporations are making substantial profits and they owe them to the black community. The black community is their *margin of profit,* yet these corporations do not do business with us."

REVEREND AL SHARPTON
The Man Behind the Sound Bite, 1990

"Black men and women need to create their own economic base. Without economic power there is no political power."

LUTHER CAMPBELL
As Nasty as They Wanna Be, 1992

"As African-Americans, we must continue to instill in our children a desire to actively participate in the economic development of the black community. . . ."

EARL GRAVES
The Daily News, February 27, 1994

"We don't educate our children early enough about money matters but if we want economic empowerment, we need to first control the dollars."

CASSANDRA MILLS
Ebony, April 1994

Ø *Education* Ø

"Education is the development of power and ideal. We want our children trained as intelligent human beings should be, and we will fight for all time against any proposal to educate black boys and girls simply as servants and underlings, or simply for the use of other people. They have a right to know, to think, to aspire."

W. E. B. DuBois
August 1906

"You go to school, you study about the Germans and the French, but not about your own race. I hope the time will come when you study black history too."

Booker T. Washington
1915

"When you control a man's thinking, you do not have to worry about his actions. You do not have to tell him not to stand here or go yonder. He will find his 'proper place' and will stay in it. You do not need to send him to the back door. He will go without being told. In fact, if there is no back door, he will cut one for his special benefit. His education makes it necessary."

Carter G. Woodson, Ph.D.
The Mis-Education of the Negro, 1933

"We want education that teaches us our true history and our role in the present-day society."

Black Panther Party Platform
1966

"Parents have become so convinced that educators know what is best for children that they forget that they themselves are really the experts."

MARIAN WRIGHT EDELMAN
Psychology Today, June 1975

"I just won't buy the idea that a Negro can't get a decent education unless he's in an integrated situation."

GUICHARD PARRIS
Certain People: America's Black Elite, 1977

"Schooling is what happens inside the walls of the school, some of which is educational. Education happens everywhere, and it happens from the moment a child is born—and some people say before—until it dies."

SARA LAWRENCE LIGHTFOOT
A World of Ideas, 1989

"We've got to turn this backward thinking around where ignorance is champion over intelligence. Young black kids being ridiculed by their peers for gettings As and speaking proper English: That's criminal."

SPIKE LEE
Newsweek, November 16, 1992

"If southern whites found the prospect of an educated slave so threatening, education must hold the promise of liberation."

AUDREY EDWARDS and DR. CRAIG K. POLITE
Children of the Dream: The Psychology of Black Success, 1992

"In the nineties we're confronted with a ghettocentric mentality that thinks speaking proper English is 'acting white,' that academic achievement is learning the 'White man's lesson,' and that blackness is synonymous with lewdness. . . . The limitations of this attitude must be held up to ridicule. It must be made unhip to be inarticulate."

NELSON GEORGE
Essence, November 1993

"Since when did learning at school become 'acting white'? Why isn't robbing, stealing, drinking, carousing, and spreading illnesses considered 'acting white'? . . . I'd rather have learning at school called 'acting black.' "

RALPH WILEY
What Black People Should Do Now, 1993

"We are in the midst of a renaissance of solid scholarship about African-American social and cultural forms. . . . The bad news is that too many black studies programs have become segregated, ghettoized amen corners of quasireligious feeling, propagating old racial fantasies and even inventing new ones."

HENRY LOUIS GATES, JR.
Essence, February 1994

∅ Equality ∅

"We must either have all the rights of American citizens, or we must be exterminated, for we can never again be slaves; nor can we cease to trouble the American people while any right enjoyed by others is denied or withheld from us. . . ."

FREDERICK DOUGLASS
1857

"If colored men get their rights and not colored women theirs, you see the colored men will be masters over the women, and it will be just as bad as it was before."

SOJOURNER TRUTH
1878

"The wisest among my race understand that the agitation of questions of social equality is the extremist folly, and the progress in the enjoyment of all the privileges that will come to us must be the result of severe and constant struggle, rather than of artificial forcing. . . . In all things purely social we [blacks and whites] can be separate as the fingers, yet one as the hand in all things essential to mutual progress."

BOOKER T. WASHINGTON
September 18, 1895

"If we are not striving for equality, in heaven's name for what are we living for? I regard it as cowardly and dishonest for any of our colored men to tell white people or colored people that we are not struggling for equality."

JOHN HOPE
Speech in Nashville, 1896

"The cost of liberty is less than the price of repression."

W. E. B. DuBois
John Brown, 1909

"From the day I set foot in France, I became aware of the working of a miracle within me. . . . I recaptured for the first time since childhood the sense of being just a human being."

JAMES WELDON JOHNSON
Along This Way, 1933

"Goddamit look! We live here and they live there. We black and they white. They got things and we ain't. They do things and we can't. It's just like living in jail."

RICHARD WRIGHT
Native Son, 1940

". . . If you want to indulge in some luxury for the good of your soul, why should not one race have the privilege as well as the other?"

MARIAN ANDERSON
Ebony, 1944

"We must face it, there will be some Negroes among us who will claim to prefer segregation to integration. . . . Inevitably there will be some who are just too weak, too timid, too lacking in self-confidence, too incompetent, or just too plain lazy to wish to risk competition in the open field beyond the ghetto."

RALPH BUNCHE
Ralph Bunche: An American Life, July 4, 1954

"I want to be a man on the same basis and level as any white citizen. . . . I want to exercise, and in full, the same rights as the white American. I want to be eligible for employment exclusively on the basis of my skills and employability, and for housing solely on my capacity to pay."

Ralph Bunche
Ralph Bunche: An American Life, July 6, 1962

"I believe in the brotherhood of all men, but I don't believe in wasting brotherhood on anyone who doesn't want to practice it with me. Brotherhood is a two way street."

Malcolm X
Speech at Harvard University, December 16, 1964

"My fight is not to be a white man in a black skin, but to inject some black blood, some black intelligence into the pallid mainstream of American life, culturally, socially, psychologically, philosophically."

John Oliver Killens
The New York Times, June 7, 1964

"A good many observers have remarked that if equality could come at once, the Negro would not be ready for it. I submit that the white American is even more unprepared."

Martin Luther King, Jr.
Where Do We Go From Here: Chaos or Community?, 1967

"On the road to equality there is no better place for blacks to detour around American values than in its forgoing its example in the treatment of its women and the organization of its family life."

Eleanor Holmes Norton
Sisterhood Is Powerful, 1970

∅ Fame ∅

"My fame makes the great ones of the country to bow down. . . ."

HATSHEPSUT
Circa 1423 B.C.

"The main reason I have for buying such extravagant objects (furs, jewelry, big cars) is because a Broadway star cannot dress like a waif or ride in the subway. I gotta live and appear in public as they [fans] expect me to."

ETHEL WATERS
Brown Sugar: Eighty Years of America's Black Female Superstars, 1935

"Being a star made it possible for me to get insulted in places where the average Negro could never hope to go and get insulted."

SAMMY DAVIS, JR.
Yes I Can, 1965

"Fame creates its own standard. A guy who twitches his lips is just another guy with a lip twitch—unless he's Humphrey Bogart."

SAMMY DAVIS, JR.
Yes I Can, 1965

"I'm the world champion but I don't feel any different than that fan over there. I'll still walk in the ghettoes, answer questions, kiss babies. I didn't marry a blonde or go nude in the movies. I'll never forget my people."

MUHAMMAD ALI
Sports Illustrated, November 11, 1974

"For a time, at least, I was the most famous person in the entire world."

JESSE OWENS
Jesse: The Man Who Outran Hitler, 1978

"I never wanted to be a star, I just wanted to get work."

GREGORY HINES
Newsweek, June 15, 1992

"... There's no doubt that fans are part of the life of an athlete.... I could spend twenty-four hours a day reading fan mail and responding to it, but then I wouldn't have any time left to play basketball...."

SHAQUILLE O'NEAL
Shaq Attack!, 1993

∅ Family ∅

"... Family for blacks in South Africa means everybody: grandparents, aunts, uncles, cousins, nephews, nieces, the lot. The concept of the nuclear family is foreign to us."

MARK MATHABANE
Kaffir Boy in America, 1989

"When it came to my brothers, I considered myself the luckiest girl in the world. I was everyone's buddy, the family confidante."

LATOYA JACKSON
LaToya: Growing Up in the Jackson Family, 1991

"Maurice (my brother) is one of the most talented people in the world. ... Do I love him? I don't know. Does he love me? I don't think so ... but I don't judge him because of that. He's a good person. ..."

GREGORY HINES
Newsweek, June 15, 1992

"More than any other crap that she's [LaToya] said about me, and all the lies and stuff, what really hurts me is what she has done to my mother."

JANET JACKSON
Ebony, September 1993

"I didn't fight with my brother growing up. There was a lot of love in my house. ... His death changed my whole perspective on life. It made me want to live more."

QUEEN LATIFAH
Ebony, December 1993

Ø Fathers Ø

"Of my father I know nothing. Slavery had no recognition of fathers, as none of families."

FREDERICK DOUGLASS
Life and Times of Frederick Douglass, 1892

"My father was a militant follower of Marcus Garvey's 'Back To Africa' movement. The Lansing, Michigan, equivalent of the Ku Klux Klan warned him to stop preaching Garvey's message, but he kept on, and one of my earliest memories is of being snatched awake one night with a lot of screaming going on because our home was afire."

MALCOLM X
Playboy, May 1963

"Every night when Dad went to bed, he'd put his watch, his money, his wallet, and his knife under his pillow. . . . When he got up, he would wind his watch, but he would take more time with his knife. . . . Sometimes he would oil it. He never went out without his knife."

CLAUDE BROWN
Manchild in the Promised Land, 1965

"Even though there was so little time, we feel very close to our dad. There's a special bond among us. You know, fathers just have a way of putting everything together."

ERIKA COSBY
Harper's Bazaar, June 1983

"My father, with only a second grade education, was the hardest working man I ever knew. I think I got most of my drive from him."

JAMES BROWN
James Brown: The Godfather of Soul, 1986

"My dad and I were very close friends. I could ask him questions and we would sit and talk until the wee hours of the morning."

MARVA COLLINS
I Dream a World, 1989

"On the lecture circuit, I tell a joke about my father's [Malcolm X] romanticism toward my mother around the house and how he could just break my mother's concentration with some of the funny, romantic things he used to say or do."

ATTALLAH SHABAZZ
Ebony, February 1992

"My father saw my last basketball game and that means a lot."

MICHAEL JORDAN
The New York Times, October 7, 1993

"There were times when we were broke and I knew it. Dad found a way to sacrifice a quarter for me. I must keep that natural circle of love going around for my own son."

GREGORY HINES
Essence, November 1993

"It's true. Joe Toney is my biological father but just because you bring a child into the world doesn't make you a father. . . . Philip Harrison is the one who raised me. . . . I love my father and my father is Philip Harrison. . . ."

SHAQUILLE O'NEAL
The Daily News, February 17, 1994

∅ Food ∅

"Do not eat foods that are against your health. . . . Get away from eating a lot of greasy foods and eat more vegetables and fruits."

ELIJAH MUHAMMAD
How to Eat to Live, 1972

"Preparing food, then serving it really turns me on."

ESTHER PHILLIPS
Jet, January 29, 1976

"We [Bill Robinson and I] were what you call habitual eaters. There was a man used to make some stuff we called 'slung dung': That consisted of everything the bakers had left over—pie crusts, doughnuts. You could get a whole lot for a cent."

LEMMEUL EGGLESTON
Mr. Bojangles: The Biography of Bill Robinson, 1988

"The most distinctive of southern soups are marked by their African choice of ingredients: peanut, eggplant, and gumbo."

WILLIAM D. PIERSON
Black Legacy: America's Hidden Heritage, 1993

"I love to create recipes and cook and watch people enjoy my food. One night recently I ended up cooking for a crowd and made all kinds of things—greens, potato salad, sautéed garlic chicken, cajun catfish, pasta, chili, and German chocolate cake."

PATTI LABELLE
McCalls, April 1994

∅ Freedom ∅

"... In every human breast, God has implanted a principle which we call love of freedom; it is impatient of oppression and pants for deliverance...."

PHILLIS WHEATLEY
February 11, 1774

"I have nothing more to offer than what General Washington would have had to offer had he been taken by the British and put to trial by them. I have adventured my life in endeavoring to obtain the liberty of my countrymen and I am a willing sacrifice to their cause.... I beg, as a favour, that I may be immediately led to execution. I know that you have pre-determined to shed my blood. Why then all this mockery of a trial?"

GABRIEL PROSSER
August 1800

"We must and shall be free I say, in spite of you. You may do your best to keep us in wretchedness and misery, to enrich you and your children, but God will deliver us from under you. And wo, wo, will be to you if we have to obtain our freedom by fighting."

DAVID WALKER
Walker's Appeal, September 28, 1829

"Those who profess to favor freedom, and yet depreciate agitation, are men who want crops without plowing up the ground."

FREDERICK DOUGLASS
Speech in Canandaigua, New York, August 3, 1857

"There is no easy walk to freedom anywhere and many of us will have to pass through the valley of the shadow of death again and again before we reach the mountaintop of our desires."

NELSON MANDELA
1953

"There are Negroes who will never fight for freedom. . . . There are Negroes who will seek profit for themselves from the struggle. . . . No one can pretend that because a people may be oppressed, every individual member is virtuous and worthy."

MARTIN LUTHER KING, JR.
Why We Can't Wait, 1964

"We been saying freedom for six years and we ain't got nothin. What we gonna start saying now is 'Black Power!' "

STOKELY CARMICHAEL
June 16, 1966

"We know that the road to freedom has always been stalked by death."

ANGELA DAVIS
Daily World, August 25, 1971

"With our necklaces and matchsticks, we will liberate South Africa."

WINNIE MANDELA
April 1986

Ø God Ø

"... Our Creator is the same and never changes despite the names given Him by people here and in all parts of the world."
> GEORGE WASHINGTON CARVER
> 1907

"Seems like God don't see fit to give the black man nothing but dreams—but He did give us children to make them dreams seem worthwhile."
> LORRAINE HANSBERRY
> *A Raisin in the Sun,* 1959

"Only God has kept the Negro sane."
> FANNIE LOU HAMER
> *We Are Not Afraid,* 1962

"People see God every day, they just don't recognize him."
> PEARL BAILEY
> *The New York Times,* November 26, 1967

"The standard practices of religious worship would have us believe that God is an authoritarian master who sits in punitive judgment of our daily lives in much the same way that a tyrannical father would."
> JULIA A. BOYD, PH.D.
> *In the Company of My Sisters,* 1993

∅ Hair ∅

"Most black women still fry their hair in pathetic mimicry of the stringy texture of white women's tresses, when anybody knows [who has ever chanced to see] that there is nothing so beautiful as a colored woman's freshly washed hair."

NATHAN HARE
The Black Anglo-Saxons, 1965

"Hair has always been a very important factor in the lives of black people in the United States. Because of its importance, one of black America's early fortunes was built upon the desire by masses of black women to have straight hair."

GERALDYN HODGES MAJOR
Black Society, 1976

"My blackness has never been in my hair. Blackness is not a hairstyle."

BERTHA K. GILKEY
I Dream a World, 1989

"There was nothing . . . that I had ever wanted as much as I wanted to grow an afro. Watching the Jackson 5 on TV, Bert and I were mesmerized by Michael's enormous, fluffy helmet of hair bouncing as he bopped. . . . Dad had always refused: 'My sons aren't gonna look like stupid, raggedy-ass niggers.' "

JAKE LAMAR
Bourgeois Blues, 1991

"I am sometimes troubled that too many of us make snide and cruel comments about the politically, professional, or socially acceptable way to wear our hair."

A'LELIA PERRY BUNDLES, Great-Great-Granddaughter of Madam C. J. Walker
May 1992

"Shameful attitudes about hair often begin at home. Within the family, black parents need to teach their sons and daughters that though hair comes in a variety of textures, there is no such thing as good or bad hair. If you got hair, good!"

KATHY RUSSELL
The Color Complex, 1992

"Yeah, I took Sinead out. I've got a bald bass player. Why not a bald date?"

ARSENIO HALL
Essence, November 1993

∅ Harlem ∅

"Here in Manhattan is not merely the largest Negro community in the world, but the first concentration in history of so many diverse elements of Negro life."

ALAIN LOCKE
The New Negro, 1925

"On Sugar Hill . . . Harlem's would-be 'sassiety' goes to town."

ADAM CLAYTON POWELL, JR.
New York Post, March 28, 1935

"All of Harlem is pervaded by a sense of congestion, rather like the insistent, maddening, claustrophobic pounding in the skull that comes from trying to breathe in a very small room with all the windows shut."

JAMES BALDWIN
Notes of a Native Son, 1955

"I was in love with Harlem long before I got there. . . . Had I been a rich young man, I would have bought a house in Harlem and built musical steps up to the front door, and installed chimes that at the press of a button played Ellington tunes."

LANGSTON HUGHES
The Big Sea, 1963

"The small town of black Harlem, though surrounded by hostility, was crowded with togetherness, love, human warmth, and neighborliness. Southern Negroes fled from physical lynchings and West Indians from economic lynchings. They met in the land north of 110th Street and they brought with them their speech patterns, folkways, mores, and their dogged determination. . . . In this climate everyone knew everyone else."

LOFTEN MITCHELL
Freedomways, 1964

"Harlem Negroes do not act like the culturally deprived people of the statistical surveys but like cosmopolites. They dress like people who like high fashion and like to be surrounded by fine architecture."

HOLLIS LYNCH
The Black Urban Condition, 1973

"Most of what we know about Harlem, most of what we have been told about Harlem, has been told by people who have never lived there, or even been through there at less than 75 miles an hour."

GIL NOBLE
Jet, May 3, 1979

"The Cotton Club—Harlem's gaudiest and best-known night-spot—was virtually unknown to Afro-Americans. What began in 1918 as the Douglas Club and turned in 1920 into prize-fighter Jack Johnson's Club Deluxe, reopened in the fall of 1923 as a white sanctuary. W. C. Handy himself was turned away one evening while the sound of his music blared inside."

DAVID LEVERING LEWIS
When Harlem Was in Vogue, 1981

∅ Hatred ∅

"When our thoughts—which bring actions—are filled with hate against anyone, Negro or white, we are in a living hell. That is as real as hell will ever be."

GEORGE WASHINGTON CARVER
December 13, 1911

"Hatred, which could destroy so much, never failed to destroy the man who hated and this was an immutable law."

JAMES BALDWIN
Notes of a Native Son, 1955

"You shouldn't hate white people. You shouldn't hate anyone. That's no way to live."

MEDGAR EVERS
1963

"You lose a lot of time hating people."

MARIAN ANDERSON
The New York Times, April 18, 1965

"I once hated whites. I hated them so much that my nostrils would dilate at the sight of an Afrikaner. . . . Blind hatred so consumed me that it almost killed me. I knew I had to find a way to rise above hate. . . ."

MARK MATHABANE
Kaffir Boy in America, 1989

∅ History ∅

"You never knew what it is to be a slave; to be entirely unprotected by law or custom; to have the laws reduce you to the condition of a chattel, entirely subject to the will of another. You never exhausted your ingenuity in avoiding the snares, and eluding the power of a hated tyrant; you never shuddered at the sound of his footsteps, and trembled within hearing of his voice."

HARRIET BRENT JACOBS
Incidents in the Life of a Slave Girl, 1861

"I will not stop here to inquire whose duty it was—whether that of the white ex-master who had profited by unpaid toil, or the northern philanthropist whose persistence brought on the crisis, or the national government whose edict freed the bondmen . . . but I insist it was the duty of someone to see that those workingmen [freed slaves] were not left alone and unguided without capital, without land, without skill, without economic organization, without even the bald protection of law, order, and decency. . . ."

W. E. B. DUBOIS
The Souls of Black Folk, 1903

". . . Honest students of history can recall the day when Egypt, Ethiopia, and Tumbuktu towered in their civilizations, towered above Europe, towered above Asia. When Europe was inhabited by a race of cannibals, a race of savages, naked men, heathens and pagans, Africa was peopled with a race of cultured black men who were masters in art, science, and literature: men who were cultured and refined: men who it was said, was like the gods."

MARCUS GARVEY
1923

"In the context of the Negro problem neither whites nor blacks, for excellent reasons of their own, have the faintest desire to look back; but I think that the past is all that makes the present coherent, and further, that the past will remain horrible for exactly as long as we refuse to assess it honestly."

JAMES BALDWIN
Notes of a Native Son, 1955

"History is a people's memory, and without a memory, man is demoted to the lower animals."

MALCOLM X
1964

"During the Reconstruction, other stereotypes were added to those of the contented slave, the comic minstrel, and the wretched freedman. These were the brute Negro and the tragic mulatto."

STERLING A. BROWN
The Massachusetts Review, 1966

"How did the Egyptians see themselves? They painted themselves in three colors: black, reddish-brown, yellow. The color white was available to them, but they used it to portray blue-eyed, white-skinned foreigners."

LERONE BENNETT, JR.
Before the Mayflower: A History of Black America, 1982

". . . It is sometimes assumed that the typical female slave was a houseservant—either a cook, maid or mammy. . . . As is so often the case, the reality is actually the diametrical opposite of the myth . . . seven out of eight slaves, men and women alike, were field workers."

ANGELA Y. DAVIS
Women, Race & Class, 1983

"If there is one thing about the history of the Tuskegee Airmen that is as unmistakable as the silhouette of a P-51, it is the fact that *these were not ordinary people.* . . . They brooked no opposition to their goals, accepted no shortcuts. . . . Courage, Character, Determination, Drive. . . . These are the things that made up their character."

> COLIN POWELL
> *Colin Powell,* August 1991

"We need to haunt the halls of history and listen anew to the ancestors' wisdom."

> MAYA ANGELOU
> *The New York Times,* August 25, 1991

"Unfortunately for African-American health care, many paternalistic masters tried to prohibit use of the herbal medicines, preferring to offer instead their own or a local white doctor's purges, emetics, tonics, or ointments."

> PROFESSOR WILLIAM D. PIERSON
> *Black Legacy: America's Hidden Heritage,* 1993

"History is a clock that people use to tell the cultural and political time of day. It is also a compass that people use to find themselves on the map of human geography."

> DR. JOHN HENRI CLARKE
> *The Daily News,* February 27, 1994

"Black history means a lot . . . a whole lot. It lets the world know what the black man has done. My wife, Nuffie, says we should celebrate it every day, and I agree."

> CAB CALLOWAY
> *The Daily News,* February 27, 1994

"Nat Turner's insurrection was a landmark in the history of slavery.... It was the forerunner of the great slavery debates, which resulted in the abolition of slavery in the United States...."

W. S. Drewry
Before the Mayflower: A History of Black America, 1982

∅ Humor ∅

"No wonder the whites after five centuries of contact, could not understand our race when out of [a] melancholy environment the blacks could create . . . high laughter."

CLAUDE MCKAY
1928

"If you want to feel humor too exquisite and subtle for translation, sit invisibly among a gang of Negro workers."

W. E. B. DuBois
1940

"Humor is laughing at what you haven't got when you ought to have it."

LANGSTON HUGHES
The Book of Negro Humor, 1966

"I try to keep my humor away from the specific 'black' and make it pertain to the general 'human.' "

BILL COSBY
Jet, October 19, 1967

"The difference between me and other black comics is that they talk *to* white people. I talk *about* them."

PAUL MOONEY
Jet, August 2, 1993

"Southerners survived because we never lost the ability to laugh at ourselves and we certainly have never stopped laughing at white folk."

LAUREN ADAMS DELEON
Emerge, December/January 1994

∅ Image ∅

"Prince has got that raunchy thing, almost like a pimp and a bitch all wrapped up in one image . . . but he's really like his name . . . a prince of a person when you get to know him."

MILES DAVIS
Miles: The Autobiography, 1989

"I make an active effort to remain a positive role model to kids. They need people to show them there's another way."

M. C. HAMMER
1991

"Just because you see black people in sitcoms, it doesn't mean it's going to be honest. We have to watch out for the images that they're putting out. Some of these things just wind up being minstrel shows. . . . The only thing is you don't have to put the makeup on now."

BILL COSBY
April 30, 1992

"I like the image Michael [Jordan] has made for himself, an image of a good guy who gets involved in the community, likes kids, has a lot of self-confidence, but isn't just some crazy egomaniac."

SHAQUILLE O'NEAL
Shaq Attack!, 1993

"It sometimes hurts me that people may think I'm a bitchy diva. . . . That's not who I am."

MARIAH CAREY
Ebony, April 1994

∅ Jail ∅

"I was in prison before entering here. . . . The solitude, the long moments of meditative contemplation, have given me the key to my freedom."

Malcolm X
Letter from prison, July 25, 1949

"Some people have asked me how I can do this when I am expecting my first child but this will be a black child born in Mississippi and thus wherever he is born he will be in prison. . . . The time has come, and is indeed long past, when each of us must make up his mind, when arrested on unjust charges, to serve his sentence and stop posting bonds. . . . We in the nonviolent movement have been talking about jail without bail for two years or more. It is time for us to mean what we say. . . ."

Diane Nash
We Are Not Afraid, April 1962

"I was accused of robbing a gas station of $70. . . . I agreed to confess in return for a light county jail sentence. . . . They tossed me into the penitentiary with one to life. That was in 1960. I was eighteen years old. I've been here ever since."

George Jackson
Soledad Brother: The Prison Letters of George Jackson, June 10, 1970

"The whole thing [jail] is calculated to destroy you, not only morally but also physically."

Winnie Mandela
October 1970

"We must not forget and we must continue to struggle for the hundreds and thousands of sisters and brothers who still languish in jails throughout the U. S. We must continue our efforts until they all are free."

ANGELA DAVIS
Jet, March 9, 1972

"Jails and prisons are designed to break human beings, to convert the population into specimens in a zoo—obedient to our keepers, but dangerous to each other."

ANGELA DAVIS
Angela Davis: An Autobiography, 1974

"If every state had to pay workers to do the jobs prisoners are forced to do, the salaries would amount to billions. License plates alone would amount to millions. . . . Prisons are a profitable business. . . . In every state, more and more prisons are being built and even more are on the drawing board. Who are they for? They certainly aren't planning to put white people in them."

ASSATA SHAKUR
Assata: An Autobiography, 1987

∅ Jews ∅

"In every black ghetto, Jews own the major businesses. Every night the owners of these businesses go home with that black community's money. . . . I doubt that I have ever uttered this absolute truth . . . without being hotly challenged and accused by a Jew of anti-Semitism. Why?"

MALCOLM X
Malcolm X Speaks, 1963

"One of the more unprofitable strategies we could ever adopt is to join in history's oldest and most shameful witch hunt, anti-Semitism . . . it is nonsense to divert attention from who it is that really oppresses Negroes in the ghetto. Ultimately the real oppressor is white American immorality and indifference and we will be letting off the real oppressor too easily if we now concentrate our fulminations against a few Jews. . . . To engage in anti-Semitism is to engage in self-destruction."

BAYARD RUSTIN
New York Amsterdam News, April 8, 1967

"No one has ever heard the Jews publicly chant a slogan of Jewish power, but they have power. Through group identity, determination, and creative endeavor, they have gained it. . . . This is exactly what we must do."

MARTIN LUTHER KING, JR.
Where Do We Go from Here: Chaos or Community?, 1968

"I'm totally bored with hearing the history of Jewish involvement in the civil-rights movement. I'm only interested in what's possible now."

MELANIE LOMAX, Attorney
Broken Alliance: The Turbulent Times Between Blacks and Jews in America, 1988

"Three hundred Hasidic Jews stormed the [police] precinct in Williamsburg [Brooklyn] because a rabbi had been arrested by the police. . . . This outburst which caused the physical injury of forty-nine police officers was met with absolutely nothing . . . no one was arrested, no warning shots were fired, nothing was done."

REVEREND AL SHARPTON
The Man Behind the Sound Bite, December 6, 1990

"Anti-Semitism is a horrible thing but just as all criticsm of blacks is not racism, so not every negative comment about Jews . . . is anti-Semitism. To leap with a vengeance on inflammatory comments by blacks is a misguided effort to vent justified fears on black targets who are the society's least powerful influences and . . . the most likely to be made the scapegoats for deeply rooted anti-Semitism that they didn't create and that will not be cured by their destruction."

DERRICK BELL
Faces at the Bottom of the Well, 1992

"I have no reason to feel anything but affection and respect for Jews as a people in the United States. . . ."

ARTHUR ASHE
Days of Grace, 1992

"The present impasse in black–Jewish relations will be overcome only when self-critical exchanges take place within and across black and Jewish communities, not simply about their own group interest, but also and more importantly, about what being black or Jewish means in ethical terms."

CORNEL WEST
The Daily News, March 27, 1994

∅ Laws ∅

"We [blacks] are entitled to a member of the Supreme Court. We never had a member and probably never will; but we have kept quiet. . . . We are entitled to thirteen United States senators, according to justice and our numerical strength, but we have not one. . . ."

CONGRESSMAN GEORGE WHITE
1899

"I think Brown v. Board of Education demonstrates that law can also change social patterns. Provided it is adequately enforced, law can change things for the better; moreover, it can change the hearts of men; law has an educational function also."

SUPREME COURT JUSTICE THURGOOD MARSHALL
1954

"An unjust law is a code that a numerical or power majority group compels a minority group to obey but does not make binding on itself. . . . One who breaks an unjust law must do so openly, lovingly, and with a willingness to accept the penalty."

MARTIN LUTHER KING, JR.
Why We Can't Wait, 1963

"We want all black people when brought to trial to be tried in court by a jury of their peer group of people from their black communities, as defined by the Constitution of the United States. . . . A peer is a person from a similar economic, social, religious, geographical, environmental, historical, and racial background."

BLACK PANTHER PARTY PLATFORM
1966

"Peaceful picketing carried on in a location open generally to the public is protected by the First Amendment."

SUPREME COURT JUSTICE THURGOOD MARSHALL
1968

"According to U. S. law, all [of the Haitian refugees] were entitled to a hearing and this step was routinely denied them."

ARTHUR ASHE
Days of Grace, 1992

∅ Leaders ∅

"There is many a leader of our race who tells us that everything is well, and that all things will work out themselves and that a better day is coming. Yes, all of us know that a better day is coming; we all know that one day we will go home to Paradise, but whilst we are hoping by our Christian virtues to have an entry into Paradise, we also realize that we are living on earth, and that the things that are practiced in Paradise are not practiced here."

MARCUS GARVEY
1923

"Leadership should be born out of the understanding of the needs of those who would be affected by it."

MARIAN ANDERSON
The New York Times, July 22, 1951

"I have no Messiah complex and I know that we may need many leaders to do the job. . . . Let us not succumb to divisions and conflicts. The job ahead is too great."

MARTIN LUTHER KING, JR.
Let the Trumpet Sound, June 1960

"The potential black leadership looks at the pitiable condition of the black herd: the corruption, the preoccupations with irrelevance, the apparent ineptitude concerning matters of survival. . . . He weighs this thing that he sees in the herd against the possible risks he'll be taking at the hands of the fascist monster and he naturally decides to go for himself, feeling that he can't help us because we are beyond help, that he may as well get something out of existence."

GEORGE JACKSON
Soledad Brother: The Prison Letters of George Jackson
April 4, 1970

"... For little crumbs of power, black preachers [in the 1940s] and other leaders could be counted on to 'keep the natives in line' ... to preach that blacks should clean up their own backyards rather than challenge the system."

J. L. CHESTNUT, JR.
Black In Selma, 1990

"There has been a corruption of the public estate, a disregard by those on top for those fundamental values that would hold us together."

SHARON PRATT DIXON
Inaugural Address, January 2, 1991

"Leaders at all levels of society—politicians, activists, teachers, intellectuals, entrepreneurs—must be held accountable and operate in the best interest of the people they serve. . . . When they fail to operate in this manner, they must be exposed for their opportunism and the basis of their legitimacy withdrawn."

TIFFANY PATTERSON, Essayist
Why L. A. Happened, 1993

"I come from a base of angry people who need me to articulate their grievances."

REVEREND AL SHARPTON
The Daily News, February 13, 1994

"People respond to any strong leader who is clear about what he stands for and has a following of people with a great deal of fervor."

REPRESENTATIVE MAJOR R. OWENS (D-Brooklyn)
The New York Times, March 5, 1994

∅ Love ∅

". . . There ain't nothing an old man can do for me except bring me a message from a young one."
JACKIE "MOMS" MABLEY
1940s

". . . Even after we began to have dates, Medgar remained slightly aloof. . . . He didn't even try to kiss me until we had been out together a number of times."
MYRLIE B. EVERS
For Us, the Living, 1967

"In real love you want the other person's good. In romantic love you want the other person."
MARGARET ANDERSON
The Fiery Fountains, 1969

"Everybody's the same when it comes to love. . . . When someone in the ghetto falls in love she hears bells, the same bells someone uptown hears when she falls in love."
BERRY GORDY, Jr.
Rolling Stone, February 1, 1973

"Love is like playing checkers. You have to know which man to move."
JACKIE "MOMS" MABLEY
Black Stars, May 1973

"Love is a special word, and I use it only when I mean it. You say the word too much and it becomes cheap."
RAY CHARLES
Brother Ray: Ray Charles' Own Story, 1978

"Love is misery."

> MARVIN GAYE
> *Jet*, January, 1983

"He didn't belong to me. He was the people's man. I never had the dreams of a young girl falling head over heels with a Prince Charming. There was no time for that."

> WINNIE MANDELA
> 1984

"... In many ways you become who you love...."

> PATRICE GAINES
> *The Washington Post*, February 23, 1992

"If you are looking for love, prepare yourself to give and receive it."

> SUSAN TAYLOR
> *Essence*, February 1994

"Love means trust, friendship, respect...."

> LOVIE HALL
> *Ebony*, February 1994

∅ Luck ∅

"I consider myself luckier than most."

JAMES BROWN
James Brown: The Godfather of Soul, 1986

"I say luck is when an opportunity comes along and you're prepared for it."

DENZEL WASHINGTON
Jet, November 9, 1987

"I don't believe in luck. . . . It's persistence, hard work, and not forgetting your dream."

JANET JACKSON
Ebony, September 1993

". . . You are lucky if you even find just some happiness."

MYRA JOHNSON
The New York Times, March 2, 1994

Ø Manhood Ø

"There is no manhood future in the United States for the Negro. He may eke out an existence for generations to come, but he can never be a man—full, symmetrical and undwarfed."

> BISHOP HENRY M. TURNER
> *The Black West,* 1895

"Rise, Brothers! Come let us possess this land. Never say: 'Let well enough alone.' Cease to console yourselves with adages that numb the moral sense. Be discontented. . . . Let your discontent break mountain-high against the wall of prejudice, and swamp it to the very foundation. Then we shall not have to plead for justice nor on bended knee crave mercy; for we shall be men."

> JOHN HOPE
> Speech in Nashville, Tennessee, 1896

"Black men, you were once great; you shall be great again. Lose not courage, lose not faith, go forward. The thing to do is to get organized; keep separated and you will be exploited, you will be robbed. You will be killed. Get organized, and you will compel the world to respect you."

> MARCUS GARVEY
> 1923

"The American black man has to make it or lose it in America; he has no choice. That's why I wrote *Cotton Comes to Harlem.*"

> CHESTER HINES
> 1964

"No man or group of men have been more denuded of their self-respect, none in history have been more terrorized, suppressed, repressed, and denied male expression than the U. S. black."

GEORGE JACKSON
Soledad Brother: The Prison Letters of George Jackson
June 28, 1968

"The black man always surfaces with his manhood not only intact but much more intact than that of his oppressor."

JEAN CAREY BOND and PATRICIA PEERY
Liberator, May 1969

"I'm not crazy for pretty men. Beauty in a man is not a weakness of mine."

TINA TURNER
I, Tina, 1986

"Who's raising black men in this country? Black women. So if black men are not being very conscious of black women then it is our fault."

BERTHA K. GILKEY
I Dream a World, 1989

"I'm concerned about what's happening to African-American males in this country."

DANNY GLOVER
People, August 16, 1993

∅ *Marriage* ∅

"I got me a good wife. Had all good wives. Loved 'em all. . . ."
JOE LOUIS
1964

"With children no longer the universally accepted reason for marriage, marriages are going to have to exist on their own merits."
ELEANOR HOLMES NORTON
Sisterhood Is Powerful, 1970

"My first marriage was a good one but sometimes you come to a dead end in a marriage and you have to let go. Letting go is love, too, you know."
BOBBY WOMACK
Jet, January 29, 1976

"I think marriage is a partnership and I think give and take should be 50 percent on both sides."
JAYNE KENNEDY
Jet, November 26, 1981

"Marriage is miserable unless you find the right person that is your soulmate and that takes a lot of looking."
MARVIN GAYE
1983

". . . You work to make a successful marriage. It isn't just enough to be the breadwinner and for your wife to be a caring and supportive helpmate. You have to *talk*: husband to wife, man to woman, human being to human being."
REGGIE JACKSON
Reggie, 1984

"He's my husband, my companion, my lover, my confidant. But not my focus. I wasn't lost and then found Arne. I was single and met a wonderful man and we enjoyed each other's company . . . so it was not lost and found. That's crap."

DIANA ROSS
You, April 16, 1989

"One marries many times at many levels within a marriage. If you have more marriages than you have divorces within the marriage, you're lucky. . . ."

RUBY DEE
I Dream a World, 1989

"Frances was the best wife I ever had and I made a mistake when I broke up with her."

MILES DAVIS
Miles: The Autobiography, 1989

"Marriage is not totally separated from what we call romantic love, but such love is never seen as the foundation for marriage."

MARGO JEFFERSON and ELLIOTT P. SKINNER
Roots of Time: A Portrait of African Life and Culture, 1990

"Just looking at my parents' marriage . . . was enough to lead both Michael and me to conclude that we would never wed. Who needed the grief?"

LATOYA JACKSON
LaToya: Growing Up in the Jackson Family, 1991

"When people ask me how we've lived past 100, I say 'Honey, we were never married. We never had husbands to worry us to death.' . . . In those days, a man expected you to be in charge of a perfect household, to look after his every need. Honey, I wasn't interested."

BESSIE DELANEY
Having Our Say: The Delaney Sisters' First 100 Years, 1993

"It feels good being married, but I never thought I'd be married. . . . I never thought I would because my parents got divorced and it gives you a different attitude about that type of thing."

MARIAH CAREY
Ebony, April 1994

∅ Media ∅

"From the press ... we have suffered much by being incorrectly represented. ... Our vices and our degradation are ever arrayed against us, but our virtues are passed by unnoticed."

JOHN B. RUSSWORM
Freedom's Journal, March 16, 1827

"The Negro press is not only one of the most successful business enterprises owned and controlled by Negroes; it is the chief medium of communication which creates and perpetuates the world of make believe for the black bourgeoisie. ... Its exaggerations concerning the economic well-being and cultural achievements of Negroes, its emphasis upon Negro 'society' all tend to create a world of make believe into which the black bourgeoisie can escape from its inferiority and inconsequence in American society."

E. FRANKLIN FRAZIER
Black Bourgeoise, 1962

"The media's the most powerful entity on earth. ... They have the power to make the innocent guilty and to make the guilty innocent, and that's power. Because they control the minds of the masses."

MALCOLM X
Malcolm A To X, 1963

"During those days [1950s], no one in America was closer to the pulse of colored life than the society editors of the black press. Through their columns and news items about the most intimate phases of black life, they did more to interpret the social patterns of the community than the sociologists or psychologists."

GERALDYN HODGES MAJOR
Black Society, 1976

"Whenever the media talks about him [Jesse Jackson], it becomes a black and white issue as opposed to the contributions he can make to this country."

STEVIE WONDER
Jet, May 30, 1988

"Many interviewers when they come to talk to me, think they're being progressive by not mentioning in their stories any longer that I'm black. I tell them, 'Don't stop now. If I shot somebody you'd mention it.' "

COLIN POWELL
Colin Powell, February 1991

"Over the years media hype would have us believe that women have elevated their positions and earning power considerably because of the women's movement. Unfortunately, the media's image is clearly out of focus, targeting only a very small percentage of women, most of whom are white and middle class."

JULIA A. BOYD
In the Company of My Sisters, 1993

"Criticism, even when you try to ignore it, can hurt. I have cried over many articles written about me, but I move on and I don't hold on to that. . . ."

DIANA ROSS
Secrets of a Sparrow, 1993

"The media coverage and commentary attempted to paint the riot that followed the [Rodney King] verdict as a *Black Reac-*

tion, but the images and newspaper coverage make it clear that the rioting included white and latino participants."

TIFFANY PATTERSON, Essayist
Why L. A. Happened, 1993

"Knowing that the [*Sports Illustrated*] swimsuit issue has been put out for the last thirty years, it appalls me that they have not been able to find a black woman beautiful enough to put on the cover."

ROSHUMBA
The Daily News, February 27, 1994

"In recent issues of popular black magazines, black writers have gone through lengthy gyrations trying to justify using the 'N' word. . . . They missed the point. Words are not value-neutral. . . . They reflect society's standards. The word 'nigger' does precisely that; it is the most hurtful and enduring symbol of black oppression."

EARL OFARI HUTCHINSON
Upscale, April 1994

Ø Military Ø

"It is more than unfortunate, it is an injustice, that regiments that have distinguished themselves in the way the 10th Cavalry and the 25th Infantry have done, should be reduced from combat service to be menials to white regiments, without chance for training and promotion and be excluded from other branches of the services. It is merely a pretense that Negroes are accorded the same treatment in the United States Army as is given white troops. It never has been the case and is not now so."

MAJOR ROBERT RUSSA MOTON
Letter to President Herbert Hoover, September 17, 1931

"We demand the abolition of segregation and discrimination in the Army, Navy, Marine Corps, Air Corps and all other branches of national defense."

A. PHILIP RANDOLPH
1942

"We want all black men to be exempt from military service. . . ."

BLACK PANTHER PARTY PLATFORM
1966

"Somebody kept trying to tell me everything was going to be all right because I'd most likely be brought in [to World War II] as a musician and wouldn't have to do any fighting. But I told them I wasn't going anywhere. I said I ain't going to take all that training and stuff. I ain't going out on them maneuvers jumping in foxholes with them goddamn snakes and things out there in them swamps. I said I wouldn't and I meant that."

COUNT BASIE
Good Morning Blues, 1985

"We must be certain that our armed forces remain strong . . . that they always have what is needed to accomplish their mission."

COLIN POWELL
Colin Powell, 1989

"The U. S. Constitution is a remarkable document—and a demanding one for those of us who choose to make our career in the military. We are required to pledge our sacred honor to a document that looks at the military as a necessary but undesirable institution useful in times of crisis and to be watched carefully at all other times."

COLIN POWELL
U. S. News and World Report, February 4, 1991

Ø Money Ø

"We have money among us, but how much of it is spent to bring deliverance to our captive brethren?"

FRANCIS HARPER
The Anglo-African, May 1859

"My object in life is not simply to make money for myself or to spend it on myself. I love to use a part of what I make in trying to help others."

MADAM C. J. WALKER
1912

"Where there is money, there is fighting."

MARIAN ANDERSON
Marian Anderson, A Portrait, 1941

"Money it turned out was exactly like sex; you thought of nothing else if you didn't have it and thought of other things if you did."

JAMES BALDWIN
Nobody Knows My Name, 1961

"I'm broke.... I'm not particularly fond of money."

MARVIN GAYE
Jet, January 1983

"Black folks with money have always tended to support candidates who they believed would protect their financial interests."

ASSATA SHAKUR
Assata: An Autobiography, 1987

"Without money, you have no control. Without control, you have no power."

SPIKE LEE
Business Week, August 6, 1990

"I don't believe that I personally have been changed by the money.... The bad thing is people *assume* you've changed because now you have money."

SHAQUILLE O'NEAL
Shaq Attack!, 1993

"Money is at the root of every mess you can think of, including slavery...."

BESSIE DELANEY
Having Our Say: The Delaney Sisters' First 100 Years, 1993

∅ Mothers ∅

"My only recollections of my own mother are of a few hasty visits made in the night on foot, after the daily tasks were over."

FREDERICK DOUGLASS
Life and Times of Frederick Douglass, 1892

"Throughout all her bitter years of slavery [my mother] managed to preserve a queenlike dignity."

MARY MCLEOD BETHUNE
1911

". . . My mother's ardently religious disposition dominated the household. . . ."

RICHARD WRIGHT
Black Boy, 1937

"My mother used to have all of these home remedies she would make herself. . . . She was very big on hot toddys."

WILMA RUDOLPH
1960

"My mother is one of the most courageous people I have ever known, with an uncanny will to survive."

ABBEY LINCOLN
Negro Digest, September 1966

"My mother believed in freedom and equality even though we didn't know it for reality during our life in Alabama."

ROSA PARKS
I Dream a World, 1989

"Role model? My mother leads the pack. . . . I regard her as I do all of the other black women throughout history: miraculous."

CICELY TYSON
I Dream a World, 1989

"I was not a very good mother. I don't have those nurturing mommy skills that you need."

WHOOPI GOLDBERG
Ebony, March 1991

"My mother was always very fair. . . . She let me do what I had to do . . . even when we couldn't see eye to eye on things, we could at least discuss them."

QUEEN LATIFAH
Ebony, December 1993

"My mother has always been more of the business side of the family. She had a kind of 'Get up and go get it' attitude."

MICHAEL JORDAN
Ebony, December 1993

"She was always a caring person. [Once] a guy came to our back door and it was freezing cold. Mom gave him one of our good coats."

ZINA GARRISON JACKSON
USA Weekend, January 30, 1994

∅ Music ∅

"Slaves were expected to sing as well as to work. A silent slave was not liked, either by masters or overseers."

FREDERICK DOUGLASS
Life and Times of Frederick Douglass, 1892

"Negro bands like plenty of brass and it is as the result of this influence that many white bands which formerly utilized a single trombone and two trumpets are now using two trombones and three trumpets or cornets. . . ."

DUKE ELLINGTON
Cincinnati Enquirer, June 5, 1932

"A dark man shall see dark days. Bop comes out of them dark days. Folks who ain't suffered much cannot play bop, neither appreciate it."

LANGSTON HUGHES
Simple Takes a Wife, 1953

"Commercial rock and roll music is a brutalization of one stream of contemporary Negro church music . . . an obscene looting of a cultural expression."

RALPH ELLISON
Shadow and Act, 1964

"So Elvis Presley came, strumming a weird guitar and wagging his tail across the continent, ripping off fame and fortune as he scrunched his way, and, like a latter-day Johnny Appleseed, sowing seeds of a new rhythm and style in the white soul of the new white youth of America, whose inner hunger and need was no longer satisfied with the antiseptic white shows and whiter songs of Pat Boone."

ELDRIDGE CLEAVER
Soul on Ice, 1968

"Music is the greatest communication in the world. Even if people don't understand the language that you're singing in, they still know good music when they hear it."

LOU RAWLS
Jet, August 26, 1976

"My music is sensual and it deals with a lot of romantic things. . . . They aren't just baby you done me wrong songs."

LUTHER VANDROSS
Ebony, December 1991

". . . Anything a young black musician does that's instrumental is going to be seen as jazz. . . ."

DON BYRON, Musician
The New York Times Magazine, January 16, 1994

"Black Music is the pop music of the '90s."

JANINE MCADAMS, *Billboard*, editor
"Black History 1993," Channel 7 WABC-TV, January 23, 1994

"I'm going to make an assault on the country music business. I've always had a love for this music. And now that I'm fifty-two years old, I'm going to do what I want."

CHUBBY CHECKER
Jet, January 31, 1994

"There are no wrong notes."

THELONIOUS MONK

"Music is your own experience—your thoughts, your wisdom. If you don't live it, it won't come out of your horn."

CHARLIE PARKER

"You've got to find some way of saying it without saying it."

DUKE ELLINGTON

"... Street rap is an unforgivable and unspeakable obscenity that some black entertainers have enriched themselves on by selling music that describes women as 'bitches and hos,' other blacks as 'niggers,' and encourages wanton violence against women and the police."

EARL G. LONG
Upscale, April 1994

∅ Old Age ∅

"The man who views the world at fifty the same as he did at twenty has wasted thirty years of his life."

MUHAMMAD ALI
Playboy, November 1975

"How old would you be if you didn't know how old you was?"

SATCHEL PAIGE
The New York Times, June 8, 1984

"I will never give in to old age until I become old. And I'm not old yet!"

TINA TURNER
I, Tina, 1986

"... For a while in your life you worry about the passage of time and getting old and so forth, and after a while you just say, 'my God, does it matter? ...'"

BOBBY SHORT
Jet, May 30, 1988

"Great fringe benefits come with the approach of senior citizenship. Young people defer to you, presuming that your age has brought you great wisdom. And older people smile at you because you, like them, have been around, outliving wars, earthquakes, scourges, and pestilence."

EARL G. GRAVES
Black Enterprise, July 1991

"... Even with all my wrinkles! I am beautiful!"

BESSIE DELANEY
Having Our Say: The Delaney Sisters' First 100 Years, 1993

"I'm a full woman at fifty—full of knowledge, full of love, full of compassion. . . . Some people get that at an earlier age, but at fifty I'm just beginning to get it, and I'll be even better at sixty."

PATTI LaBELLE
McCalls, April 1994

"I've lived so long because I get my rest and I take my time. The one thing I try to tell people is to slow down, don't be in such a rush."

MARY THOMPSON, Age 118
National Enquirer, April 5, 1994

∅ *Oppression* ∅

"We of this less-favored race realize that our future lies chiefly in our hands. . . . And we are struggling on, attempting to show that knowledge can be obtained under difficulties. . . . Neither the old-time slavery, nor continued prejudice need extinguish self-respect, crush manly ambition or paralyze effort."

PAUL ROBESON
1919

"Don't be afraid of the Klan! Quit running! Hold your head up high. Look every man straight in the eye and make no apology to anyone because of . . . color."

MARY McLEOD BETHUNE
1920

"It is my business not only to tell the guy with the whip hand to go easy on my people but also to teach my people—all oppressed people—how to prevent that whip hand from being used against them."

PAUL ROBESON
1939

"If . . . plumbing for the truth reveals within the Negro personality, homicidal mania . . . a pathetic sense of inferiority . . . arrogance . . . Uncle Tomism . . . hate and fear and self-hate . . . this then is the effect of oppression on the human personality."

CHESTER HIMES
1948

"All token blacks have the same experience. I have been pointed at as a solution to things that have not *begun* to be solved, because pointing at us token blacks eases the conscience of millions, and I think this is dreadfully wrong."

LEONTYNE PRICE
Divas: Impressions of Six Opera Superstars, 1959

"When you respect the intelligence of black people in this country as being equal to that of whites, then you'll realize that the reaction of the black man to oppression will be the same as the reaction of the white man to oppression."

MALCOLM X
1963

"I grew up in a small, segregated southern town, but the oppression there was nothing compared to the oppression I saw in the big-city black ghetto."

WILMA RUDOLPH
1967

"Black people already know they're poor and powerless. They just don't understand the nature of their oppression. They haven't drawn the line from their condition to the *system* of capitalism."

HUEY P. NEWTON
1970

"Racial oppression of black people in America has done what neither class oppression or sexual oppression with all their perniciousness, has ever done: destroyed an entire people and their culture."

ELEANOR HOLMES NORTON
Sisterhood Is Powerful, 1970

"The oppression of women, like the oppression of blacks, is one of the pillars of the capitalist system of exploitation. The fight to weaken any one of these pillars contributes to weakening the entire structure that victimizes us all."

WILLIE MAE REID
International Socialist Review, March 1975

"We turned the other cheek so often our heads seemed to revolve on the end of our necks like old stop-and-go signs. . . . We forgave as if forgiving was our talent."

MAYA ANGELOU
The Heart of a Woman, 1981

"I got into heated arguments with sisters or brothers who claimed that the oppression of black people was only a question of race. I argued that there were black oppressors as well as white ones. That's why you've got blacks who support Nixon or Reagan or other conservatives. Black folks with money have always tended to support candidates who they believed would protect their financial interests."

ASSATA SHAKUR
Assata: An Autobiography, 1987

"Our black lesbian and bisexual sisters are sisters without cause or exception and deserve the same honor and respect that we all deserve. When we place ourselves in a position of judgment, then we turn ourselves into oppressors."

JULIA A. BOYD
In the Company of My Sisters, 1993

Ø *Patriotism* Ø

"We Negroes love our country. We fought for it. We ask only that we be treated as well as those who fought against it."

PAUL LAURENCE DUNBAR
August 25, 1893

"One ever feels his twoness—an American, a Negro; two souls, two thoughts, two unreconciled strivings; two warring ideals in one dark body, whose dogged strength alone keeps it from being torn asunder."

W. E. B. DUBOIS
The Souls of Black Folk, 1903

"This is the greatest country under the sun but we must not let our love of country, our patriotic loyalty cause us to abate one whit in our protest against wrong and injustice."

MADAME C. J. WALKER
August 1917

"The making of an American begins at that point where he himself rejects all other ties, any other history and himself adopts the vesture of his adopted land."

JAMES BALDWIN
Notes of a Native Son, 1955

Ø Performing Ø

"What success I achieved in the theater is due to the fact that I have always worked just as hard when there were ten people in the house as when there were thousands. Just as hard in Springfield, Illinois as on Broadway."

BILL "BOJANGLES" ROBINSON
New York Daily Mirror, December 15, 1936

"The first time I sang it [*Strange Fruit*] I thought it was a mistake. There wasn't even a patter of applause when I finished. Then a lone person began to clap nervously. Then suddenly everyone was clapping."

BILLIE HOLIDAY
1945

"I'm a musician at heart, I know I'm not really a singer. I couldn't compete with real singers. But I sing because the public buys it."

NAT "KING" COLE
Nat King Cole, 1949

"Singing the old spirituals for blacks who are not ashamed of being black or from the South helps me fight for my people."

MAHALIA JACKSON
1963

"Duke Ellington never grinned. He smiled. Ellington never shuffled. He strode. It was 'Good afternoon, ladies and gentlemen,' never 'How y'all doin?' At his performances we [blacks] sat up high in our seats."

GORDON PARKS
Mom, The Flag and Apple Pie, 1976

"Every dancer lives on the threshold of chucking it."
JUDITH JAMISON
The New York Times Magazine, December 5, 1976

"I don't think I'll do any serious acting; *48 Hours* is about as heavy as I want to get."
EDDIE MURPHY
Newsweek, January 3, 1983

"I've sung *Oo oo Baby Baby* maybe 10 trillion times, but every time I sing that song, I still feel what's happening."
SMOKEY ROBINSON
Jet, September 24, 1984

"I sing about life."
MARVIN GAYE
Jet, 1984

"While my brothers and I were paying dues on the so-called chitlin' circuit, opening for other acts, I carefully watched all the stars because I wanted to learn as much as I could."
MICHAEL JACKSON
Jet, May 16, 1988

"Acting is the one thing I always knew I could do."
WHOOPI GOLDBERG
Ebony, March 1991

"I feel that when I go onstage and dance it's not just me dancing, it's Honi Coles and Sandman Sims and Teddy Hale and Baby Lawrence. . . . I get very emotional about it."
GREGORY HINES
Newsweek, June 15, 1992

"You know, most of the film roles out there for us are hookers, drug dealers' girlfriends, strippers in a club, that type of thing. So it's frustrating. But it's getting better."

HALLE BERRY
New Woman, November 1993

"White America has always let us entertain them but we've never had any real control, any real power. . . . It's a new day you know, and it's time for us to stop shooting the ball and start owning the court."

ARSENIO HALL
Essence, November 1993

"I enjoy belting out a song and singing all those wonderful romantic songs. I also enjoy changing into beautiful clothes."

DIAHANN CARROLL
The Daily News, April 10, 1994

∅ Police ∅

"As of 1970, the highest-ranking blacks in New York's police department were all West Indians, as were all black federal judges in the city."

THOMAS SOWELL
Ethnic America, 1981

"They ought to pick more fair-minded people to be police officers, because the job's too important to have any kind of racist white person walking around with a gun and a license to kill."

MILES DAVIS
Miles: The Autobiography, 1989

"Half the time you don't trust the police because they're into crime themselves."

PAULINE CLAYTON, Teacher, Brooklyn, New York
The New York Times, January 4, 1994

"...Remember something called the Mollen Commission? You had cops telling how they snorted cocaine off the dashboard in cruisers, then looked for citizens who were not white to beat up...."

EARL CALDWELL, Columnist
The Daily News, January 21, 1994

Ø Politics Ø

"Let the Afro-American depend on no party, but on himself for his salvation."

IDA B. WELLS
The New York Age, November 11, 1892

"Who are the nonvoters? By and large, they are poor and low-income people, including Negroes. They are the people who get the worst deal in this society. On the other hand, those who vote generally have higher incomes and better educations. They get the best deal—which is why they vote. They have their stake and they mean to keep it."

BAYARD RUSTIN
New York Amsterdam News, September 21, 1968

"Even old Moms couldn't do nothin' for the man [Richard Nixon], 'cept give him a few licks upside the head. . . . He was just too far gone."

JACKIE "MOMS" MABLEY
1970s

"We know we have to have political clout if we want economic empowerment. And we have that clout if we mobilize the black vote. . . . There are 17 million blacks of voting age: but only 10 million are registered and only 7 million vote."

JOHN E. JACOB, President
National Urban League, July 31, 1983

"There are powerful incentives to continue the political crusades of the past, even after their beneficial effects are exhausted. Part of the reason is inertia. A large civil-rights establishment, inside and outside government, has to find work to do. . . ."

THOMAS SOWELL
The Economics and Politics of Race, 1983

"Nonvoting is a fruitless temper tantrum."
> BRUCE WRIGHT
> *Black Robes, White Justice,* 1987

"We must now refocus the views of the public on the issue of justice rather than the issues of aimless harmony."
> REVEREND AL SHARPTON
> June 21, 1990

"Black mayors are expected to control black crime, particularly that affecting whites."
> DERRICK BELL
> *Faces at the Bottom of the Well,* 1992

"I think that this [confirmation] hearing today is a travesty. . . . The Supreme Court is not worth it . . . And from my standpoint as a black American, it is a high-tech lynching for uppity blacks who in any way deign to think for themselves."
> JUDGE CLARENCE THOMAS
> October 11, 1992

"I endured the personal humiliation of being vilified as a madwoman with strange hair—you know what that means—a strange name and strange ideas, like democracy, freedom, and fairness that mean all people must be equally represented in our political process."
> LANI GUINIER
> *Jet,* August 2, 1993

"What a bitter twist of fate. This black man [Judge Clarence Thomas] who had, in hustling the favors of Bush and the right-wingers who currently controlled America—and who had disparaged and ridiculed Thurgood Marshall, Walter White, James Weldon Johnson, Roy Wilkins, and others who wiped out lynching—was now crying 'lynching' to justify his confirmation. This child of Georgia poverty who had ... exhorted blacks never to fall back on cries of 'racism' was shouting 'racist lynching' in the most galling of ways."

CARL T. ROWAN
Dream Makers, Dream Breakers, 1993

"Mayor Giuliani [of New York City] says blacks have a fear of his administration. On that, he's right. He says he does not know the reason blacks feel the way they do. On that, he's got to be kidding. . . ."

EARL CALDWELL
The Daily News, January 21, 1994

"I . . . am calling on the Black Caucus, the N.A.A.C.P., Reverend Jackson, and the Rainbow Coalition, black churches, and black leaders to review their relationship with the A.D.L. [Anti-Defamation League] in view of its wickedness against our people."

LOUIS FARRAKHAN
The New York Times, February 4, 1994

"If I run [for Congress], it will be because I want to bring a better representation to this [Harlem] district, better accountability, and better leadership. . . ."

ADAM CLAYTON POWELL, IV
The New York Times, February 27, 1994

"While I believe that independent politics is where the black community and others need to go, the Democratic Party is where they are."

DR. LENORE FULANI
New York Amsterdam News, March 5, 1994

∅ *Poverty* ∅

"Are there any so stupid as to believe these outrages have been . . . heaped upon the Negro because he is black? Not at all. It is because he is poor. It is because he is dependent. Because he is poorer as a class than his white wage-slave brother of the North."

LUCY PARSONS, Activist
1886

"I cannot understand how he can put together all those programs for sending food across the oceans when at home we have people who are slowly starving to death. We could use less foreign aid and more home aid."

PEARL BAILEY
Pearl's Kitchen, 1973

"If you talk to a deprived child of any kind, they're not talking about upscale . . . they're thinking about food and shelter. . . . That is the difference between those who have and those who have not."

LOU GOSSETT
Upscale, 1994

∅ Power ∅

"Power concedes nothing without a demand. It never did and it never will. . . ."

FREDERICK DOUGLASS
Speech in Canandaigua, New York, August 3, 1857

"The Negro will have to build his own government, industry, art, science, literature, and culture before the world willstop to consider him. Until then, we are but wards of a superior race and civilization, and the outcasts of a standard social system."

MARCUS GARVEY
1923

"Since the black bourgeoisie is composed chiefly of white-collar workers and since its small-business enterprises are insignificant in the American economy, the black bourgeoisie wields no political power as a class in American society."

E. FRANKLIN FRAZIER
Black Bourgeoise, 1962

"The civil-rights direction of protest is dead. Now we must concentrate on control—economic and political power."

MARION BARRY
Speech to constituents, Washington, D. C., January 1967

"Too much agreement kills a chat."

ELDRIDGE CLEAVER
Soul on Ice, 1968

"The black middle class [dreams] of building black economic and political power with the support and cooperation of the white power structure. . . ."

GRADE LEE BOGGS
November 12, 1968

"Groups have surfaced demanding 'white power' as though the locus of power had ever been with the blacks."

BRUCE WRIGHT, Supreme Court Justice
Black Robes, White Justice, 1987

"America has become comfortable and literally color-blind in its acceptance and adoration of the blacks who entertain, but it is still stubbornly racist in conceding equitable power to blacks in most other arenas. That shouldn't be surprising. The power to entertain is not quite the same as the power to control."

AUDREY EDWARDS and DR. CRAIG K. POLITE
Children of the Dream: The Psychology of Black Success, 1992

Ø Public Figures Ø

"Madame C. J. Walker's life was the clearest demonstration I know, of a Negro woman's ability recorded in history. She has gone, but her work still lives and shall live as an inspiration to not only her race but to the world."

MARY McLEOD BETHUNE
May 25, 1919

"Elijah Muhammad has been able to do what generations of welfare workers and committees and resolutions and reports and housing projects and playgrounds have failed to do: to heal and redeem drunkards and junkies, to convert people who have come out of prison and to keep them out, to make men chaste and women virtuous, and to invest both the male and the female with a poise and a serenity that hang about them like an unfailing light."

JAMES BALDWIN
The Fire Next Time, 1963

"The die is set and Malcolm shall not escape . . . such a man is worthy of death."

LOUIS FARRAKHAN
The Final Call, 1965

"If you knew him you would know why we must honor him: Malcolm was our manhood, our living black manhood! This was his meaning to his people. And in honoring him, we honor the best in ourselves. . . . However much we may have differed with him or with each other about him and his value as a man, let his going from us serve only to bring us together, now. . . . And we will know him then for what he was and is—

---

a prince—our own black shining prince who didn't hesitate to die, because he loved us so."

OSSIE DAVIS
Eulogy for Malcolm X, 1965

"More than anything else I would like to be like Nat 'King' Cole. He had staying power, something that all people, no matter what color, liked."

LOU RAWLS
Jet, August 26, 1972

"There's a pure beauty to Grace Jones.... That face of hers is like a chiseled ebony statue."

BILLY DEE WILLIAMS
Jet, September 10, 1984

"She is an honest, hardworking woman who has developed an unusual amount of caring and courage. Oprah Winfrey is making her journey at what might seem to be a dizzying pace, but it is her pace. She has set her own tempo."

MAYA ANGELOU
Ms., January/February 1989

"I was deeply saddened to learn of the death of my dear friend, Sammy Davis, Jr.... In mourning his passing, we also celebrate a life of great achievement, compassion, and commitment."

CORETTA SCOTT KING
Jet, June 4, 1990

"Clarence Thomas is wrong on every possible question we can think of that is important to our future survival as a people."

PEARL CLEAGE
Deals with the Devil and Other Reasons to Riot, 1993

"... It's shocking to discover that Whoopi [Goldberg] equates a mostly Jewish audience's lampooning Billy Crystal's and Joan River's Jewishness with her white lover's repeatedly calling her nigger in public—and in a Sambo costume no less!"

PLAYTHELL BENJAMIN
The Daily News, October 15, 1993

"Congratulations to Toni Morrison [on winning the 1993 Nobel Prize in Literature]. It took the Swedes to recognize her greatness."

EDITORIAL
The City Sun, October 19, 1993

"For all his marvelous gifts, [Michael] Jordan wasn't inclined to use his visibility to carry a torch for equal rights and ending racism."

WILLIAM C. RHODEN
Emerge, December/January 1994

"Over the years, myriad surgeries have changed his features and left me confused about who he is and who he aspires to be. And I'm sorry, but after all the caucasianizing cuts, I question Michael [Jackson's] explanation that some rare pigment affliction is the reason his skin is so pale."

PAMELA JOHNSON
Essence, March 1994

∅ Racism ∅

"We have been sentenced to die for something we ain't never done. Us poor boys been sentenced to burn up on the electric chair for the reason that we is workers—and the color of our skin is black. We like any of you workers is none of us older than twenty. Two of us is fourteen and one is thirteen years old. What we guilty of? Nothing but being out of a job. Nothing but looking for work. Our kinfolk was starving for food. We wanted to help them out. So we hopped a freight just like any of you workers might a done—to go down to Mobile to hunt work. We was taken off the train by a mob and framed up on rape charges."

> THE SCOTTSBORO BOYS: ANDY WRIGHT, OLEN MONTGOMERY, OZIE POWELL, CHARLIE WEEMS, CLARENCE NORRIS, HAYWOOD PATTERSON, EUGENE WILLIAMS, and WILLIE ROBERTSON
> *The Negro Worker,* May 1932

"I got the feeling on hearing the discussion yesterday that when you put a white child in school with a whole lot of colored children, the child would fall apart or something. . . . Now is the time for this Court to make clear that is not what our Constitution stands for."

> SUPREME COURT JUSTICE THURGOOD MARSHALL
> December 1952

"Just being a Negro doesn't qualify you to understand the race situation any more than being sick makes you an expert on medicine."

> DICK GREGORY
> *Nigger,* 1964

"As if living in the sewer, learning in the streets, and working in the pantry weren't enough of a burden for millions of America Negroes, I now learn [via the Moynihan Report] that we've caught 'matriarchy' and the 'tangle of Negro pathology....'"

JAMES FARMER
1965

"If a man like Malcolm X could change and repudiate racism, if I myself and other former Muslims can change, if young whites can change, then there is hope for America."

ELDRIDGE CLEAVER
Soul on Ice, 1968

"Racism is so universal in this country, so widespread, and deep-seated, that it is invisible because it is so normal."

SHIRLEY CHISOLM
Unbought and Unbossed, 1970

"I believe racism has killed more people than speed, heroin, or cancer and will continue to kill until it is no more."

ALICE CHILDRESS
Stagebill, May 1972

"Most Negroes have a little black militancy swimming around in them and most white people have a little Ku Klux Klan swimming around in them. If we'd be honest with each other, we would discover we are all victims of the racism that is historically part of this country."

BARBARA JORDAN
Speech in Washington, D. C., 1977

"Black Haitian refugees were tossed back into the sea, and those who remained were introduced to the ghost of the Dred

Scott syndrome by having to sue for human rights in a country that invented them."

BRUCE WRIGHT
Black Robes, White Justice, 1987

"In the last twenty-five years, the stresses of new freedom, which have greatly intensified black vulnerability, have led us, I believe, to claim more racial victimization than we have actually endured."

SHELBY STEELE
The Content of Our Character, 1990

"The great movement of the '60s destroyed the brutal and visible manifestations of racism, but it did not and could not at that time destroy the invisible institutional manifestations of racism. And in 1993, there were still invisible Jim Crow signs on the walls of every American institution."

LERONE BENNETT, JR.
The Shaping of Black America, 1993

"Once you begin to explain or excuse all events on racial grounds, you begin to indulge in the perilous mythology of race. It is dangerous to say 'the white man is the cause of my problems' or 'the black man is the cause of my problem ... ' substitute any color—the danger is implicit."

JAMES EARL JONES
Voices and Silence, 1993

"To me, racism is not as hard an issue to deal with any-more ... because the laws have been changed, it doesn't threaten that many people."

BERNICE KING
The New York Times, January 20, 1994

"We can go on talking about racism and who treated whom badly, but what are you going to do about it? Are you going to wallow in that or are you going to create your own agenda?"

JUDITH JAMISON
Black Elegance, February 1994

"They don't lynch darkies in America anymore."

KEN HAMBLIN
The Daily News, February 27, 1994

∅ Religion ∅

"Religion without humanity is a poor human stuff."

SOJOURNER TRUTH
1877

"No one can say that Christianity has failed. It has never been tried."

ADAM CLAYTON POWELL, JR.
Marching Blacks, 1945

"If Christianity had asserted itself in Germany, 6 million Jews would have lived. . . ."

MALCOLM X
The Autobiography of Malcolm X, 1965

"I'm neutral on the question of Jesus. Maybe He was the son of God, maybe not. I can go either way without any trouble. . . . My relationship is really with the Supreme Being, not with Jesus."

RAY CHARLES
Brother Ray: Ray Charles's Own Story, 1978

"My opposition [to apartheid] is based firmly and squarely on the Bible and on the injunctions of the Christian gospel."

ARCHBISHOP DESMOND TUTU
The Words of Desmond Tutu, 1984

"If we can put the names of our faiths aside for a moment and look at principles, we will find a common thread running through all the great religious expressions."

LOUIS FARRAKHAN
The Final Call, December 22, 1993

"The question isn't where are the blacks in the Bible, but where are the whites?"

DR. CAIN HOPE FELDER, Howard University
Ebony, February 1994

"My ministry is not a ministry of hate. It is a ministry of love. We are teaching our people to love themselves. We're tired of laying at the feet of the white people begging them to do for us what we can do for ourselves."

LOUIS FARRAKHAN
The New York Times, February 27, 1994

∅ Revolution ∅

"I took my station in the rear and, as it was my object to carry terror and devastation wherever we went, I placed fifteen or twenty of the best armed and most to be relied on in front, who generally approached the houses as fast as their horses could run. This was for two purposes—to prevent their escape and strike terror to the [white] inhabitants."

NAT TURNER
1831

"I had reasoned this out in my mind, there was two things I had a right to: liberty and death. If I could not have one, I would have the other, for no man should take me alive."

HARRIET TUBMAN
1869

"If someone hit me on one cheek, I'd tear his head off before he could hit me on the other one."

PAUL ROBESON
1946

"Many of our white brothers . . . fail to interpret correctly the nature of the Negro Revolution. Some believe that it is the work of skilled agitators who have the power to raise or lower the floodgates at will."

MARTIN LUTHER KING, JR.
Why We Can't Wait, 1963

". . . You don't have a peaceful revolution. You don't have a turn-the-other-cheek revolution. There's no such thing as a nonviolent revolution. . . . Revolution is bloody. Revolution is hostile. Revolution knows no compromise. Revolution overturns and destroys everything that gets in its way."

MALCOLM X
Chicago Defender, November 21, 1963

∅ Sex ∅

"A woman is a woman until the day she dies, but a man's a man only as long as he can."

JACKIE "MOMS" MABLEY
1940s

"If a fellow ceases dating you because you refuse to engage in the sexual act, you can be assured that he is not genuinely interested in you and therefore would make an undesirable husband."

MARTIN LUTHER KING, JR.
Ebony, October 1958

"Marilyn Monroe and I discussed it often and agreed it would be nice if we could be strong enough in ourselves as women and not just there to make the male audience want to go to bed with us."

LENA HORNE
Jet, May 3, 1976

"The most exciting men in my life have been the men who have never taken me to bed. One can lose a great friend by going to bed with them."

EARTHA KITT
Confessions of a Sex Kitten, 1989

"Sex and racism have always been tied together. Look at the thousands of black men who got lynched and castrated. The reason the Klan came into being was to protect white southern women."

SPIKE LEE
Time, June 17, 1991

"I want everybody to practice safe sex, and that means using condoms. I want everybody to be aware of what is going on.... AIDS is really spreading in the black community...."

EARVIN "MAGIC" JOHNSON
Arsenio Hall Show, November 8, 1991

"We must change homosexual behavior and get rid of the circumstances that bring it about."

LOUIS FARRAKHAN
A Torchlight for America, 1993

"Sex is a fact of life and I am a very sexual person. Some people think big people don't have sex.... Yes, we have sex. Lots of it."

THEA VIDALE
USA Weekend, January 30, 1994

"Casual sex is the norm, not the exception on campus. More often than not, it's taken for granted by both men and women."

PLACIDA BLACKWOOD
Ebony, February 1994

"I support abstinence as much as anyone, but if I know from the facts that young people are not being abstinent ... I can't bury my head in the sand and pretend we don't have a problem."

DR. JOYCELYN ELDERS
Ebony, February 1994

Ø The Sixties Ø

"Many of the [black] Johnny-come-latelies to the [Civil Rights] Movement appear to have been moved mainly by the largely unanimous approval of the white press."

NATHAN HARE
The Black Anglo-Saxons, 1965

"Today it is the Negro artist who does *not* speak out who is considered to be out of line."

PAUL ROBESON
1965

"On April 4 [1968], King was shot and the rioting began again, worse than ever. Praying, waiting, singing, and everything white were out. Rioting was viewed as urban guerrilla warfare, the first step toward the complete overthrowing of the honky, racist government. On the cultural level everything had to be rehauled. Black poems, plays, paintings, novels, hairstyles, and apparel were springing up like weeds in Central Park."

MICHELE WALLACE
Black Macho and the Myth of the Superwoman, 1975

"When people made up their minds that they wanted to be free and took action, then there was a change. . . ."

ROSA PARKS
I Dream a World, 1989

"The impact of them killing Medgar Evers hit me so hard . . . I cried for the first time in years."

LENA HORNE
I Dream a World, 1989

"I grew up watching the '60s on TV. . . . I watched, more in mystification than in horror, white policemen on horseback charging into a crowd of black people on the Edmund Pettus bridge. I watched ghettos burning to the ground."

JAKE LAMAR
Bourgeois Blues, 1991

"Whenever I had to go into one of these southern towns, I didn't want the authorities to immediately know that [Martin Luther] King's man was in town. . . . We decided that the most effective way to get the attention of the deciders and presiders of Birmingham was to stop the ebb and flow of finance. . . . We wanted a boycott that would be 50 percent effective among blacks. It was more than 90 percent effective. You couldn't *find* any blacks downtown."

REVEREND WYATT TEE WALKER
Free at Last?, 1991

"The [Black Panther] party's platform and program was a declaration and an outline for black empowerment. It demanded resitution for slavery, food, education, decent housing, and land for black people. . . . It demanded the exemption of blacks from the military service, the release of all black prisoners, and the granting of new trials by juries of their peers."

ELAINE BROWN
A Taste of Power, 1992

"People were going to bed Negro and waking up black. There were major psychological changes going on."

DR. RON BROWN
Children of the Dream: The Psychology of Black Success, 1992

"It was thrilling to be able to challenge the circumstances in which black people were confined: to mobilize and raise consciousness, to change the way people saw themselves, blacks could express themselves. . . . It gives you an unshakable confidence in your ability. . . ."

ELAINE BROWN
The New York Times Magazine, January 31, 1993

∅ Sports ∅

"I made a lot of mistakes out of the ring, but I never made any in it."

JACK JOHNSON
1910

"I looked about me [on the day of the big fight July 4, 1910] and scanned that sea of white faces. I felt the auspiciousness of the occasion. There were few men of my own race among the spectators. I realized that my victory in this event meant more than on any previous occasion. It wasn't just the championship that was at stake—it was my own honor—and in a degree, the honor of my race. I was well aware of all these things and I sensed that most of that great audience was hostile to me but I was cool and perfectly at ease. I never had any doubt of the outcome."

JACK JOHNSON
1915

"I could hear them [black fans] shouting in the stands, and I wanted to produce so much that I was tense and overanxious. . . . I started swinging at bad balls and doing a lot of things I would not have done under ordinary circumstances. I wanted to get a hit for them because they were pulling so hard for me."

JACKIE ROBINSON
April 20, 1946

"Until the time comes when a Negro player can go out and argue his point as well as any other ball player, I hope that all of us are able to bite our tongues and just play ball."

JACKIE ROBINSON
Ebony, June 1948

"Sports and politics do mix. Behind the scenes, the two are as inextricably interwoven as any two issues can be. I'm sure politics are involved when teams get franchises or when cities build stadiums. It is unrealistic to say you shouldn't bring politics into sports."

ARTHUR ASHE
The New York Times, October 6, 1977

". . . Big league baseball can be a cold business. It's not like college ball. My first three months with the Padres were just about the hardest months in my life. The older players were not about to help me out. Everybody was fighting for a job on the team . . . and I was there taking a job away from some veteran. Everybody was very cool and distant."

DAVE WINFIELD
Dave Winfield: The 23 Million Dollar Man, 1982

"In sports, especially professional sports, your accomplishments only stand up on their own when you retire."

DARRYL STRAWBERRY
Darryl, 1992

"I've been called the Jackie Robinson of golf by many newspaper writers over the years but . . . I'm a little disgusted by the comparison at this point in my life. It's true that I was the first black to break into the all-white PGA tour. . . . Out of nearly 400 professional golfers in this country, there are only seven blacks? That's so far out of line that it's ridiculous."

CHARLIE SIFFORD
Just Let Me Play, 1992

"My main focus is basketball. I want to win an NBA title."

LARRY JOHNSON
Ebony, March 1994

"... In terms of playing, you can never have too many re-bounders and good defensive players on your team. That's the New York Knicks' identity: guys who rebound, guys who play hard.... Those are all the qualities that I have."

ANTHONY BONNER
The New York Times, March 6, 1994

∅ Success ∅

"In these strenuous times, we are likely to become morbid and look constantly upon the dark side of life, and spend entirely too much time considering and brooding over what we can't do, rather than what we can do, and instead of growing morose and despondent over opportunities that are shut from us, let us rejoice at the many unexplored fields in which there is unlimited fame and fortune to the successful explorer. . . ."

GEORGE WASHINGTON CARVER
1908

"Except when they [the Negro professionals] are talking within the narrow field of their profession, their conversations are generally limited to sports—baseball and football. They follow religiously the scores of the various teams and achievements of all the players. For hours they listen to radio accounts of sports and watch baseball and football games over television."

E. FRANKLIN FRAZIER
Black Bourgeoisie, 1957

"The ultimate of being successful is the luxury of giving yourself the time to do what you want to do."

LEONTYNE PRICE
Newsday, February 1, 1976

"I don't know the key to success, but the key to failure is trying to please everybody."

BILL COSBY
Ebony, June 1977

"Whether or not you reach your goals in life depends entirely on how well you prepare for them and how badly you want them. . . . You're eagles! Stretch your wings and fly to the sky!"

RONALD MCNAIR, Astronaut
Speech at Howard University, 1983

"Whenever I need inspiration, I listen to people like Duke Ellington, Charlie Parker, and Miles Davis. My goal is to be like them. But I'm not at that level yet—no way."

WYNTON MARSALIS
Jet, September 10, 1984

". . . Success comes from within and Bill was determined to be something."

MRS. ANNA COSBY
The Cosby Book, 1986

"If you are unhappy with anything—your mother, your wife, your job, your boss, your car—whatever it is bringing you down, get rid of it. . . ."

TINA TURNER
I, Tina, 1986

"Just don't give up trying to do what you really want to do. . . . Where there's love and inspiration, I don't think you can go wrong."

ELLA FITZGERALD
1987

"There are no secrets to success: Don't waste time looking for them. Success is the result of perfection, hard work, learning from failure, loyalty to those for whom you work, and persistence. . . ."

COLIN POWELL
Colin Powell, 1989

"To be successful as a black man in this country, you have to be bicultural. White people can function in a white world and only concern themselves with white things. But a black man has to know it all."

ARSENIO HALL
Arsenio, 1989

"Think that you, a single mother without a job, can be a success, and success will follow."

SUSAN TAYLOR
The Daily News, January 30, 1994

"For everyone of us that succeeds, it's because there's somebody there to show you the way out. The light doesn't necessarily have to be in your family; for me it was teachers and school."

OPRAH WINFREY
The Star, April 5, 1994

∅ Truth ∅

"Truth could move multitudes with untutored language."
    CARTER G. WOODSON, PH.D.
    1930

"The greatest and most immediate danger of white culture is its fear of the truth, its childish belief in the efficacy of lies as a method of human uplift."
    W. E. B. DUBOIS
    Dusk of Dawn, 1940

"Truth pressed to earth will rise again . . . no lie can live forever. . . ."
    MARTIN LUTHER KING, JR.
    The New York Times, March 26, 1965

"Truth is a theory that is constantly being disproved. Only lies, it seems, go on forever."
    EARTHA KITT
    Confessions of a Sex Kitten, 1989

"I had to tell the truth."
    ANITA HILL
    Newsweek, October 21, 1991

∅

∅ Unity ∅

". . . It has always been the one ideal of my life to be the greatest good to the greatest number of my people."
GEORGE WASHINGTON CARVER
April 12, 1896

"Two months ago I had a nice apartment in Chicago. I had a good job. I had a son. When something happened to the Negroes in the South I said 'that's their business, not mine.' Now I know how wrong I was. The murder of my son has shown me that what happens to any of us, anywhere in the world, had better be the business of us all."
MAMIE BRADLEY
October 1955

"The Negro's relationship with one another is utterly deplorable. The Negro wants to be everything but himself. He wants to be a white man. He processes his hair. Acts like a white man. He wants to integrate with the white man, but he cannot integrate with himself or with his own kind. The Negro wants to lose his identity because he does not know his identity."
ELIJAH MUHAMMAD
Black Nationalism, 1962

"I feel blacks should stick together economically the way Jewish people do, the way Italian people do, the way Mormons do, and others. It's something we should aim toward."
REGGIE JACKSON
Reggie, 1984

"The longer we waste time in frivolous division, this will happen again and again. . . ."
LOUIS FARRAKHAN
At the funeral of Yusuf Hawkins, August 30, 1989

"Judge [Clarence] Thomas is hoping that in taking on this victim's role, he will appeal to the black community's sense of solidarity. . . . Anita Hill is also one of our own. If her story is true, and I believe it is, she is the victim, and Clarence Thomas must not be allowed to use our collective racial victimization to blind us to that awful truth."

PROFESSOR CHARLES R. LAWRENCE III
Los Angeles Times, October 15, 1991

"To build a nation, you can't do it individually, we have to work cooperatively."

BROTHER KENNETH 6X
The New York Times, March 5, 1994

∅ Violence ∅

"It is not true, as so many commentators have said, that Nat Turner initiated a wave of violence in Southampton. The violence was already there. Slavery was violence. Nat Turner's acts . . . were responses to that violence."

LERONE BENNETT, JR.
Before the Mayflower, 1962

"For all the strength of my opposition to apartheid, I deplore all the violence that has taken place in South Africa including not only the violence of the police, the African National Congress, and the Inkatha or Zulu group."

ARTHUR ASHE
Days of Grace, 1992

"We want to make Reverend King's philosophies live on, and now the challenge is black-on-black violence."

BRIDIE F. JOYNER
King Center for Conflict Mediation
The New York Times, January 17, 1994

∅ War ∅

"One of the best evidences of confidence in the valor of colored troops is manifest in the fact that they are entrusted with holding the right of our line. . . . Their character for fighting and discipline is established."

CAPTAIN THOMAS MORRIS CHESTER
Thomas Morris Chester: Black Civil War Correspondent
September 7, 1864

"If, tomorrow, a war should arise, I would not raise a musket to defend a country where my manhood is denied."

REPRESENTATIVE HENRY MacNEAL TURNER
The Black West, 1868

"The hate and scorn heaped upon us as Negro officers by our Americans [during World War I] at Camp Mencou and Vannes, in France convinced me there was no sense of dying in a world ruled by them. . . . They boarded us off from our fellow white officers. They made us eat on benches in order to maintain segregation, and they destroyed our prestige in front of French officers."

CHARLES HOUSTON
Former First Lieutenant 368th Infantry
The Pittsburgh Courier, March 19, 1960

"We will not fight and kill other people of color in the world. . . ."

BLACK PANTHER PARTY PLATFORM
1966

"Black people are the people who fight wars for this country against other people of color around the world. Recent examples are Vietnam and Grenada."

HAKI R. MADHUBUTI
Nommo: A Literary Legacy of Black Chicago, 1986

"From A Shau [in South Vietnam] we would go out for weeks and months at a time and just live in the jungle, looking for Vietcong. It was a needle in a haystack at that time. They could find us more easily than we could find them. We were getting ambushed every morning."

Colin Powell
Colin Powell, 1992

"My feelings about Vietnam are that we never should have gotten in, we did not get out gracefully, and too many black men were killed in the conflict. It was a mistake."

Sergeant Mildred Kelly
Ebony, March 1994

∅ Washington, D.C. ∅

"Washington D. C. has a higher standard of culture among people of color than in any other city."

PAUL LAURENCE DUNBAR
Harper's Weekly, January 13, 1900

"I have recently spent several days in Washington D. C. and I have never seen the colored people so discouraged and bitter as they were at that time."

BOOKER T. WASHINGTON
1913

"Most Negroes come here [to Washington D. C.] from North or South Carolina and psychologically they think they're in freedom land."

MARION BARRY
The Washington Post, July 1966

∅ Whites ∅

"Every circumstance I met with [on the slave ship] served only to render my state more painful, and heightened my apprehensions and my opinion of the cruelty of the whites."

GUSTAVUS VASSA
The Interesting Narrative of the Life of Olaudah Equiano, or Gustavus Vassa the African, 1791

"It is no more fair . . . to say that because a white man is from the South he is an enemy to the Negro than it is to say because you are a Negro you are worthless as an American citizen. . . ."

CONGRESSMAN ARTHUR MITCHELL
The Politics of Race, 1936

"The whites of considerable means have shown less and less interest in the work of the Association [for the Study of Negro Life and History] as the years have passed. They have tended to look unfavorably upon the revelation of truth as shown by scientific investigation."

CARTER G. WOODSON, PH.D.
The Mis-Education of the Negro, 1938

". . . [White] southerners are not two-faced. If they don't like you, they'll let you know it, but if they love you, they'll die for you. They won't do like some folks I know up the [North] country, smile in your face, pat you on the shoulder, then knife you in the back first chance they get. . . ."

BILL "BOJANGLES" ROBINSON
Richmond News Leader, June 21, 1938

"There is the tendency [among some black people] in the South not to trust white people. I think this is not good. It's putting white people in that category that they put us in; it's not taking people as individuals."

MARION BARRY
The Politics of Race, 1962

"When I say the white man is a devil, I speak with the authority of history. . . ."

MALCOLM X
When the Word is Given, 1963

"You gotta say this for whites, their self-confidence knows no bounds. Who else could go to a small island in the South Pacific, where there's no crime, poverty, unemployment, war or worry—and call it a primitive society."

DICK GREGORY
1964

"White Americans are not yet ready to accept Negroes as their equals. Negroes will not accept anything less. That is the collision course we're on. We're on the road to racial Armageddon."

ROY WILKINS, Executive Director, NAACP
Jet, August 26, 1976

"With more blacks and other people of color, there will be a tilt in power . . . and whites will be in the minority. It is in the best interest of white people to work harder to create better relationships with people of color so they can ensure themselves the equality that has eluded us."

REPRESENTATIVE MAXINE WATERS
Ebony, November 1992

"When you're black, being invisible to whites is a way of life. Most white people look right through black people as if they aren't there. . . ."

DARRYL STRAWBERRY
Darryl, 1992

"... Sophisticated blacks have learned that to suggest that whites are racist is not a useful exercise in the current climates—at least when talking to whites. ..."

ELLIS COSE
The Rage of a Privileged Class, 1993

"They [white people] have always recognized art and land as investments. It has taken us longer, because we have been brainwashed to believe that value lies in gold and diamonds."

JOHN SANDRIDGE
Upscale, April 1994

∅ Winning ∅

"Sometimes it's worse to win a fight than to lose."
BILLIE HOLIDAY
Lady Sings the Blues, 1956

"The winning team like the conquering army claims everything in its path and seems to say that only winning is important. Yet like getting into a college of your choice or winning an election or marrying a beautiful mate, victory is fraught with as much danger as glory...."
BILL BRADLEY
Life on the Run, 1976

"I won in high school, I won in college but I can't win in the pros, not yet anyway."
PATRICK EWING
Pro Basketball Player, *Shaq Attack!,* 1991

Ø Womanhood Ø

"If women want any rights more than they's got, why don't they just take them, and not be talking about it?"

SOJOURNER TRUTH
Speech at National Women's Rights Convention, 1850

"I want to say to every Negro woman present, don't sit down and wait for the opportunities to come.... Get up and make them!"

MADAME C. J. WALKER
1914

"Let me state here and now that the black woman in America can justly be described as slave of a slave."

FRANCIS M. BEAL
Double Jeopardy: To Be Black and Female, 1970

"... The role of Black women is to continue the struggle in concert with Black men for the liberation and determination of Blacks."

IDA LEWIS, Editor-in-Chief
Essence, July 1970

"Black women are trained from childhood to become workers and expect to be financially self-supporting for most of their lives. They know they will have to work, whether they are married or single; work to them, unlike to white women, is not a liberating goal, but rather an imposed lifelong necessity."

GERDA LERNER
Black Women in White America, 1972

"Maybe there is a part of me that is more attracted to a white woman than a black woman, but I don't believe that; besides who cares anyway, and those that do don't matter anyway."

REGGIE JACKSON
Reggie, 1984

"I'm the kind of woman that likes to enjoy herself in peace."

ALICE WALKER
The Temple of My Familiar, 1989

"Black women ain't been put on no pedestals. Nine out of every ten black women worked in the fields alongside black men. But every time we have this image of slavery, there she is, either setting the table for 'Master' or getting in his bed."

JOHNNETTA B. COLE
I Dream a World, 1989

"When I see a black woman who is truly aware of who she is, I know I am looking at heaven walking on earth."

WESLEY SNIPES
Ebony, February 1992

"I have dated women of other cultures, but I have a love for African-American women [based on] their strength and spirit."

STEVIE WONDER
Ebony, February 1992

"The role I played in *Father Hood* was actually written for a man at first and then just a woman. So for me to be able to get it was a milestone. It was the first time I got a role that hadn't been written for a black woman, just a woman."

HALLE BERRY
New Woman, November 1993

"Any woman in my life has to deal with the fact that we may finish making love and I may jump up and write down the sounds that we made, and she may hear it on my monologue the next night."

ARSENIO HALL
Upscale, April 1994

∅ Work ∅

"An ordinary day's work is two hundred pounds [of cotton]. A slave who is accustomed to picking is punished if he or she brings in a less quantity than that."

SOLOMON NORTHUP
Twelve Years a Slave, 1853

"Nothing ever comes to one, that is worth having, except as a result of hard work."

BOOKER T. WASHINGTON
Up from Slavery, 1901

"I have made it possible for many colored women to abandon the washtub for more pleasant and profitable occupations."

MADAME C. J. WALKER
1912

"I tell you one thing, I knows tobacco. I knows all de grades an' blends. I knows bright tobacco an' burley tobacco an' Kaintucky tobacco. . . . I give Mister John his start . . . I was his best hand—he say so hisse'f—an' he didn't never pay me no mo'n fifty to sebenty-five cents a day."

ELVIRY MAGEE, Worker
The Bright-Tobacco Industry, 1948

"The price one pays for pursuing any profession, or calling, is an intimate knowledge of its ugly side."

JAMES BALDWIN
Nobody Knows My Name, 1961

"It's just a job. Grass grows, birds fly, waves pound the sand. I beat people up."

MUHAMMAD ALI
The New York Times, April 6, 1977

"What works best is delegating authority, learning you cannot do everything and some people can do it better."

WILLI SMITH
Jet, November 4, 1985

"Everyday in 1964, I hit the pavement with my best 'office-looking clothes' on and a pair of high-heeled torture shoes. . . . I identified with the job and talked about 'our' company and told people what 'we' manufactured. I wasn't making two cents over lunch money and talked like I owned the place."

ASSATA SHAKUR
Assata: An Autobiography, 1987

"In the running of my own business, I have found that female managers often work smarter and harder to get the job done."

EARL G. GRAVES
Black Enterprise, August 1991

"My work requires me to think about how free I can be as an African-American woman writer in my genderized, sexualized, wholly racialized world."

TONI MORRISON
Playing in the Dark: Whiteness in the Literary Imagination
1992

"Great careers don't come without sacrifice. Something in your life will probably have to go. Decide, now, what you're willing to forfeit to get what you want."

CYDNEY SHIELDS and LESLIE C. SHIELDS
Work Sister Work, 1993

"Getting ahead in a predominantly white corporate environment can be tricky and sometimes infuriating because you
need to hold your tongue, tread lightly, and dodge the delicate
issue of race, which will face you every step of the way."

ANITA DOREEN DIGGS
Success at Work: A Guide for African-Americans, 1993

∅ Writing ∅

"The written word is the only record we will have of this our present, or our past, to leave behind for future generations. It would be a shame if that written word in its creative form were to consist largely of defeat and death."

LANGSTON HUGHES
The Crisis, June 1941

"Any writer, I suppose, feels that the world into which he was born is nothing less than a conspiracy against the cultivation of his talent. . . ."

JAMES BALDWIN
Notes of a Native Son, 1955

"To create a market for your writing you have to be consistent, professional, a continuing writer—not just a one-article or a one-story or a one-book man. Those expert vendors, the literary agents do not like to be bothered with a one-shot writer. No money in them."

LANGSTON HUGHES
Writers: Black and White, 1960

"A black woman writer who wants to write seriously about contemporary cultural issues and how they are socially constructed is faced with an almost insurmountable communication problem: If she takes a scholarly approach, she will be virtually ignored because black women have no power in that context; if she takes a colloquial 'entertainment' approach . . . then she will be read, but she will be attacked and ostracized."

MICHELE WALLACE
Heresies, 1989

"... Whereas most older black male writers deny any black influence at all—or eagerly claim a white paternity—black female authors often claim descent from other black women literary ancestors, such as Zora Neale Hurston and Ann Petry.... The 'patricide' which characterized Baldwin's and Ellison's declarations of independence from Wright has no matricidal counterpart...."

HENRY LOUIS GATES, JR.
Reading Black, Reading Feminist, 1990

"... Black people don't like unhappy endings. Perhaps we have too many."

JAMAICA KINCAID
The New York Times, April 18, 1990

"... What is most wonderful for me personally is to know that the Nobel Prize for Literature at last has been awarded to an African-American."

TONI MORRISON
Publishers Weekly, October 11, 1993

"As an essayist I don't believe in the fiction of an anonymous observer. Rather than the sham of objectivity, I think you should put your perspective up front. That's only fair to the reader."

RALPH WILEY
Essence, November 1993

"I've followed Nelson George's writing for many years with great pleasure, so it makes me proud to see him move into the world of fiction with a book as timely and powerful as *Urban Romance.*"

SPIKE LEE
New York Amsterdam News, March 5, 1994

∅ Youth ∅

"The teenagers ain't all bad. I love 'em if nobody else does. There ain't nothin' wrong with young people. Jus' quit lyin' to 'em."

JACKIE "MOMS" MABLEY
Newsday, April 6, 1947

"We have a powerful potential in our youth, and we must have the courage to change old ideas and practices so that we may direct their power toward good ends."

DR. MARY MCLEOD BETHUNE
Ebony, August 1955

"What Negro teenagers are not inclined to accept are dead-end jobs that pay little and promise no advancement or training."

BAYARD RUSTIN
The New York Times Magazine, August 13, 1967

"When you're young, the silliest notions seem the greatest achievements."

PEARL BAILEY
The Raw Pearl, 1968

"The number one thing young people in America—indeed young people around the world—have going for them is their sense of honesty, morality, and ethics. Young people refuse to accept the lies and rationalizations of the established order."

DICK GREGORY
Dick Gregory's Political Primer, 1972

"I was one of those kids, if you gave me a whole semester to do a term paper, I waited until the night before it was due to start it. Until then, I always thought I could find a way to back out of it."

LIONEL RICHIE
Lionel Richie, 1985

"One of my greatest shames is that my behavior hurt, confused, and disappointed young people, the very youth I have fought so hard to help and uplift."

MARION BARRY
The Politics of Race, 1991

"The black youngsters of today must ask black leaders: If you can't make an effort to reach, reconstruct, and save a black man [Clarence Thomas] who has graduated from Yale, how can you reach down here in this drug-filled, hate-filled cesspool where I live and save me?"

MAYA ANGELOU
The New York Times, August 25, 1991

"I think if we're going to reclaim or recapture young people, it's going to have to be through the church or spirituality."

BERNICE KING
The New York Times, January 20, 1994

"The lives of young African-Americans growing up in the inner city are so filled with life-taking situations—drugs, guns—that they need additional help to get through."

John Amos
USA Weekend, February 25–27, 1994

"Rappers are saying look at my life, look at what it's become. Kids have something to say and we should listen."

NIKKI GIOVANNI
Essence, March 1994

"It frightens me that our young black men have a better chance of going to jail than of going to college."

JOHNNIE COCHRAN, Attorney
Ebony, April 1994

Ø Biographical List Ø

Aaron, Hank
Athlete
Alexander, Karen
Fashion Model
Ali, Muhammad
Athlete/Author
Amos, John
Actor
Anderson, Margaret
Writer/Musician
Anderson, Marian
Entertainer
Angelou, Maya
Author
Ashe, Arthur
Athlete
Ashe, Jeanne Moutoussamy
Photographer/Widow of Arthur Ashe

Bailey, Pearl
Entertainer/Author
Baldwin, James
Author/Activist
Ballard, Florence
Entertainer
Barry, Marion
Former Mayor of Washington, D.C.
Basie, Count
Entertainer
Beal, Frances M.
Essayist
Bell, Derrick
Author
Benjamin, Playthell
Newspaper Columnist

Bennett, Lerone Jr.
Historian/Author
Berry, Bertice
Talk Show Host
Berry, Halle
Entertainer
Bethune, Mary McLeod
Educator/Activist
Bevel, Reverend James
Clergyman/Activist
Blackwood, Placida
College Student
Boggs, Grade Lee
Essayist
Bond, Jean Carey
Essayist
Bonner, Anthony
Athlete
Bonds, Barry
Athlete
Boyd, Julia A.
Psychologist/Author
Bradley, Bill
Former U. S. Senator
Bradley, Mamie
Mother of Emmett Till
Braxton, Toni
Singer
Bristow, Dr. Lonnie
Physician/President, American Medical Association
Brown, Claude
Author/Attorney
Brown, Elaine
Author/Activist
Brown, James
Entertainer

Brown, Dr. Ron
  Psychologist
Brown, Sterling A.
  Author
Bunche, Ralph
  Political Scientist/Educator
Bundles, A'Lelia Perry
  *Great-great-granddaughter of
    Madam C. J. Walker*
Byron, Don
  Entertainer

Caldwell, Earl
  Newspaper Columnist
Calloway, Cab
  Entertainer
Campbell, Luther
  Entertainer
Carey, Mariah
  Entertainer
Carver, George Washington
  Scientist
Castleberry, Ed
  Radio Personality
Charles, Ray
  Entertainer
Checker, Chubby
  Entertainer
Chester, Morris Thomas
  Civil War Captain
Chestnut, J. L., Jr.
  Attorney/Author
Childress, Alice
  Author
Chisolm, Shirley
  Politician/Author
Chrisman, Robert
  Author/Essayist
Clark, Ramsey
  Civil-Rights Activist
Clarke, Dr. John Henri
  Historian/Author

Clay, Cassius
  Athlete
Clayton, Pauline
  Teacher
Cleage, Pearl
  Author
Cleaver, Eldridge
  Author/Activist
Cochran, Jonnie
  Attorney
Cole, Johnetta B.
  Educator/Author
Cole, Nat "King"
  Entertainer
Collins, Janet
  Dancer
Collins, Kimberly A.
  Essayist
Collins, Marva
  Educator
Comer, James P.
  Physician
Coombs, Orde
  Author
Copage, Eric V.
  Author
Cosby, Anna
  Daughter of Bill Cosby
Cosby, Bill
  *Actor/Comedian/TV Producer/
    Philanthropist*
Cosby, Erika
  Student/Daughter of Bill Cosby
Cose, Ellis
  Journalist/Author
Crockett, George
  Congressman
Crouch, Stanley
  Musician/Columnist
Cullen, Countee
  Poet

Dash, Julie
  Filmmaker
Davis, Miles
  Entertainer
Davis, Ossie
  Entertainer
Davis, Sammy, Jr.
  Entertainer
Dee, Ruby
  Entertainer
Delaney, Bessie
  Author
DeLeon, Lauren Adams
  Magazine Columnist
Diggs, Anita Doreen
  Author/Publicist
Dixon, Sharon Pratt
  Mayor, Washington, D.C.
Douglass, Frederick
  Lecturer/Author/Activist
Drewry, W. S.
  Essayist
DuBois, W. E. B.
  Author/Educator/Activist
Dunbar, Paul Laurence
  Author
Dunham, Katherine
  Dancer

Edelman, Marian Wright
  Author/Educator
Edwards, Audrey
  Author
Eggleston, Lemmeul
  *Childhood Friend of Bill
  "Bojangles" Robinson*
Elders, Dr. Joycelyn
  *Surgeon General of the United
  States*
Ellington, Duke
  Entertainer

Ellison, Ralph
  Author
Evers, Medgar
  Civil-Rights Activist
Ewing, Patrick
  Athlete

Farmer, James
  Activist
Farrakhan, Louis
  *Leader, Nation of Islam/
  Author*
Felder, Dr. Cain Hope
  Theologian
Fields, Kim
  Actress
Fitzgerald, Ella
  Entertainer
Flanigan, Robin
  Private Citizen
Frazier, E. Franklin
  Sociologist/Author
Fulani, Dr. Lenore
  Activist/Politician

Gaines, Patrice
  Journalist
Garvey, Marcus
  Activist/Author/Lecturer
Gates, Henry, Jr.
  Scholar/Educator
Gaye, Marvin
  Entertainer
George, Nelson
  Author/Columnist/Film Producer
Gilkey, Bertha K.
  Tenants Rights Activist
Giovanni, Nikki
  Author
Glover, Danny
  Entertainer

Goldberg, Whoopi
  Entertainer
Gossett, Lou
  Actor
Graves, Earl
  Publisher of Black Enterprise
Gray, Kimi
  Social Activist
Gregory, Dick
  Comedian/Activist
Guinier, Lani
  Attorney/Lecturer

Hall, Arsenio
  Entertainer/Talk Show Host
Hall, Lovie
  Medical School Student
Hamblin, Ken
  Radio Personality
Hamer, Fannie Lou
  Activist
Hammer
  Entertainer
Hansberry, Lorraine
  Playwright
Hardaway, Anfernee
  Private Citizen
Hare, Nathan
  Author
Harper, Frances
  Activist
Hatshepsut
  Egyptian Queen
Herman, Alexis
  Assistant to President Clinton
Hill, Anita
  Attorney/Lecturer
Hines, Gregory
  Entertainer
Holiday, Billie
  Jazz Singer

Hope, John
  Activist
Horne, Lena
  Entertainer
Houston, Charles
  Lieutenant, U.S. Army
Houston, Whitney
  Entertainer
Hughes, Dorothy Pitman
  Owner, Office Supply Store
Hughes, Langston
  Author
Hurston, Zora Neale
  Author
Hutchinson, Earl Ofari
  Author

Jackson, Bo
  Athlete
Jackson, George
  Activist
Jackson, Janet
  Entertainer
Jackson, Jesse, Rev.
  *Politician/Clergyman/Author/
  Activist*
Jackson, LaToya
  Entertainer
Jackson, Michael
  Entertainer/Author
Jackson, Reggie
  Athlete
Jackson, Richard
  *Inmate, Greenhaven
  Correctional Facility*
Jackson, Zina Garrison
  Athlete
Jacob, John E.
  *President, National Urban
  League*
Jacobs, Harriet Brent
  Former Slave

Jamison, Judith
Dancer
Jefferson, Margo
Author
Johnson, Jack
Boxer
Johnson, Earvin "Magic"
Athlete
Johnson, James Weldon
Author/Lyricist
Johnson, John H.
Publisher/Editor-in-Chief of
Ebony *and* Jet
Johnson, Larry
Athlete
Johnson, Myra
College Student
Johnson, Pamela
Editor, Essence
Jones, James Earl
Author/Actor
Jordan, Barbara
Congresswoman
Jordan, Michael
Athlete
Joyce, Ella
Actress
Joyner, Bridie F.
Activist
Joyner, Florence Griffith
Athlete
Joyner-Kersee, Jackie
Athlete

Karenga, Dr. Maulana
Creator of Kwanzaa
Kelly, Mildred
Sergeant, U. S. Army
Kennedy, Florynce R.
Lawyer/Civil-Rights Activist
Kennedy, Jayne
Entertainer

Kenneth, Brother 6X
Member, Nation of Islam
King, Reverend Berniece
Minister/Daughter of Martin
Luther King, Jr.
King, Coretta Scott
Activist/Author
King, Martin Luther, Jr.
Clergyman/Civil-Rights Leader/
Author
King, Martin Luther, Sr.
Clergyman/Author
Kitt, Eartha
Entertainer
Kouyate, Mamadou
Griot (West African Musician)

LaBelle, Patti
Entertainer
Lamar, Jake
Author/Journalist
Latifah, Queen
Entertainer
Lawrence, Charles R., III
Professor of Law/Stanford
University
Lee, Spike
Film Producer/Actor/Author
Lerner, Gerda
Essayist
Lewis, David Levering
Author
Lewis, Ida
Former Editor-in-Chief, Essence
Lightfoot, Sara Lawrence
Essayist
Lincoln, Abbey
Entertainer
Locke, Alain
Author
Lomax, Melanie
Attorney/Author

Long, Earl G.
  Essayist
Louis, Joe
  Boxer
Lynch, Hollis
  Author

Mabley, Jackie "Moms"
  Comedienne
Madhubuti, Haki R.
  Author/Publisher
Magee, Elviry
  Tobacco Worker
Major, Geraldyn Hodges
  Newspaper Columnist/Author
Mandela, Nelson
  Activist/President of South Africa
Mandela, Winnie
  Activist
Marsalis, Wynton
  Entertainer/Lyricist
Marshall, Thurgood
  Supreme Court Justice
Mathabane, Mark
  Author/Lecturer
Mays, Dr. Benjamin E.
  Educator
McAdams, Janine
  Magazine Writer
McKay, Claude
  Essayist
McClester, Cedric
  Spokesman, Kwanzaa Holiday
    Expo '93
McMillan, Terry
  Author
McNair, Ronald
  Astronaut
Mills, Cassandra
  President/Black Music Division/
    Giant Records
Mitchell, Arthur
  Congressman

Mitchell, Loften
  Author
Monk, Thelonious
  Entertainer
Montgomery, Olen
  Scottsboro Boy
Mooney, Paul
  Comedian
Moore, Queen Mother
  Activist
Morrison, Toni
  Author
Moseley-Braun, Carole
  Senator
Moton, Robert Russa
  Major, U.S. Army
Muhammad, Elijah
  Founder, Nation of Islam
Murphy, Eddie
  Entertainer

Nash, Diane
  Activist
Newton, Huey P.
  Founder, Black Panther Party
Njeri, Itaberi
  Author
Noble, Gil
  Journalist
Norris, Clarence
  Scottsboro Boy
Northrup, Solomon
  Former Slave
Norton, Eleanor Holmes
  Lawyer

O'Neal, Shaquille
  Athlete
Owens, Jesse
  Athlete
Owens, Major R.
  Senator

Paige, Satchel
  Athlete
Parker, Charlie
  Entertainer
Parks, Gordon
  Author/Photographer
Parks, Rosa
  Activist
Parris, Guichard
  Private Citizen
Parsons, Lucy
  Activist
Patterson, Haywood
  Scottsboro Boy
Patterson, Tiffany
  Essayist
Payne, Dr. N. Joyce
  Educator
Peery, Patricia
  Essayist
Phillips, Esther
  Entertainer
Pierson, William D.
  Professor/Author
Pinckney, Andrea Davis
  Editor, Essence
Polite, Dr. Craig K.
  Psychologist/Author
Poussaint, Alvin F.
  Psychiatrist
Powell, Adam Clayton, Jr.
  Politician
Powell, Adam Clayton, IV
  Politician
Powell, Colin
  *Former Chairman, Joint Chiefs
    of Staff*
Powell, Ozie
  Scottsboro Boy
Prattis, P. L.
  Newspaper Columnist

Price, Leontyne
  Entertainer
Prosser, Gabriel
  Leader of Slave Revolt/Activist

Randall, Theresa
  Actress
Randolph, A. Philip
  Labor Leader/Socialist
Rangel, Charles
  Congressman
Rawls, Lou
  Entertainer
Reed, Ismael
  Author
Reid, Inez Smith
  Essayist
Reid, Tim
  Actor
Reid, Willie Mae
  Politician/Activist
Rhoden, William C.
  Magazine Writer
Richie, Lionel
  Entertainer
Robertson, Willie
  Scottsboro Boy
Robeson, Paul
  Entertainer/Activist
Robinson, Jackie
  Athlete
Robinson, Smokey
  Entertainer
Roshumba
  Fashion Model
Ross, Diana
  Entertainer
Rowan, Carl T.
  Journalist/Author/Broadcaster
Rudolph, Wilma
  Athlete

Russworm, John B.
Journalist
Rustin, Bayard
Civil-Rights Leader

Sandridge, John
Entrepreneur
Sanford, Steve
Talent Agent
Sapphire
Author/Poet
Shakur, Assata
Activist/Author
Shabazz, Attallah
Actress/Daughter of Malcolm X
Sharpton, Al
Clergyman/Activist
Shields, Cydney
Author
Shields, Leslie
Author
Short, Bobby
Entertainer
Sifford, Charlie
Athlete
Simmons, Russell
Entrepreneur
Skinner, Elliott
Author
Smith, Willi
Fashion Designer
Snipes, Wesley
Entertainer
Sowell, Thomas
Economist/Author
Speech
Entertainer
Steele, Shelby
Author/Educator
Strawberry, Darryl
Athlete

Taylor, Susan
Editor-in-Chief, Essence
Terrell, Mary Church
Activist
Thomas, Clarence
Supreme Court Justice
Thompson, Mary
Oldest Living American
Truth, Sojourner
Former Slave/Lecturer/Activist
Tubman, Harriet
Former Slave/Activist/Lecturer
Turner, Bishop Henry
Clergyman/Activist
Turner, Nat
*Activist/Leader of Slave
Rebellion*
Turner, Tina
Entertainer
Tutu, Archbishop Desmond
Clergyman/Author/Activist
Tyson, Cicely
Entertainer

Vandross, Luther
Entertainer
Vidale, Thea
Entertainer

Walker, Alice
Author
Walker, David
Writer/Civil-Rights Activist
Walker, Madam C. J.
Entrepreneur
Walker, Monica
Private Citizen
Wallace, Michele
Author
Washington, Denzel
Entertainer

Washington, Booker T.
  Lecturer/Educator
Waters, Ethel
  Entertainer
Waters, Maxine
  Congresswoman
Weems, Charlie
  Scottsboro Boy
Wells, Ida B.
  Activist
West, Cornel
  Author/Black Studies Scholar
Wheat, Alan
  Congressman
Wheatley, Phillis
  Poet
White, George
  Congressman
Whitney, Salem-Tutt
  Newspaper Columnist
Wiley, Ralph
  Essayist
Williams, Billy Dee
  Actor/Painter
Williams, Eugene
  Scottsboro Boy
Wilson, Erlene B.
  Author

Winfield, Dave
  Athlete
Winfrey, Oprah
  *Talk Show Host/Actress/TV
    Producer*
Womack, Bobby
  Entertainer
Wonder, Stevie
  Entertainer
Woodson, Carter G.
  Educator/Author/Activist
Wright, Andy
  Scottsboro Boy
Wright, Bruce
  *Supreme Court Justice (New
    York)*
Wright, Richard
  Author

X, Malcolm
  *Activist/Religious Leader/Author/
    Lecturer*

Young, Andrew
  Politician
Young, M. C.
  Entertainer

Bibliography and
∅ References ∅

BOOKS

Aaron, Hank with Lonnie Wheeler. *I Had a Hammer.* Harper Paperbacks, 1991.

Angelou, Maya. *The Heart of a Woman.* Random House, 1981.

Angelou, Maya. *I Know Why the Caged Bird Sings.* Random House, 1970.

Ashe, Arthur and Arnold Rampersad. *Days of Grace.* Alfred A. Knopf, 1993.

Bailey, Pearl. *Hurry Up America and Split.* Harcourt Brace Jovanovich, 1976.

Bailey, Pearl. *Pearl's Kitchen,* 1973.

Bailey, Pearl. *The Raw Pearl.* Harcourt Brace Jovanovich, 1968.

Bailey, Pearl. *Talking to Myself.* Harcourt Brace Jovanovich, 1971.

Baldwin, James. *Notes of a Native Son.* Beacon Press, 1990.

Basie, Count as told to Albert Murray. *Good Morning Blues.* Random House, 1985.

Bell, Derrick. *Faces at the Bottom of the Well.* Basic Books, 1992.

Bennett, Lerone, Jr. *Before the Mayflower: A History of Black America.* Penguin Books, 1982.

Blackett, R. J. M. *Thomas Morris Chester: Black Civil War Correspondent.* DaCapo Press, 1991.

Bogle, Donald. *Brown Sugar: Eighty Years of America's Black Female Superstars.* DaCapo Press, 1993.

Boyd, Julia, A., Ph.D. *In the Company of My Sisters.* Dutton, 1993.

Brotz, Howard. *Negro Social & Political Thought.* Basic Books, 1966.

Brown, Claude. *Manchild in the Promised Land.* Signet Books, 1989.

Brown, Elaine. *A Taste of Power: A Black Woman's Story.* Pantheon, 1992.

Brown, James and Bruce Tucker. *James Brown: The Godfather of Soul.* Thunder's Mouth Press, 1990.

Bundles, A'Lelia Perry. *Madam C. J. Walker.* Chelsea House, 1991.

Cade, Toni. *The Black Woman: An Anthology.* Mentor, 1970.

Cagin, Seth and Philip Dray. *We Are Not Afraid.* Macmillan, 1988.

Campbell, Luther and John R. Miller. *As Nasty as They Wanna Be.* Barricade Books, 1992.

Chapman, Abraham. *Black Voices.* Mentor, 1968.

Charles, Ray and David Ritz. *Brother Ray: Ray Charles's Own Story.* DaCapo Press, 1992.

Cleage, Pearl. *Deals with the Devil and Other Reasons to Riot.* One World/Ballantine, 1993.

Cleaver, Eldridge. *Soul On Ice.* Dell, 1992.

Comer, James P., M.D., and Alvin F. Poussaint, M.D. *Raising Black Children.* Plume, 1992.

Coombs, Orde. *Do You See My Love for You Growing.* Dodd Mead & Co, 1970.

Cooper, Ralph and Steve Dougherty. *Amateur Night at the Apollo.* HarperCollins, 1990.

Copage, Eric V. *Kwanzaa: An African-American Celebration of Cooking and Culture.* William Morrow, 1991.

Cosby, Bill. *Childhood.* Putnam, 1991.

Cose, Ellis. *The Rage of a Privileged Class.* HarperCollins, 1993.

Dash, Julie. *Daughters of the Dust.* The New Press, 1992.

Davis, Angela. *Angela Davis: An Autobiography.* International Publication, 1988.

Davis, John P. *The American Negro Reference Book.* Prentice-Hall, 1969.

Davis, Miles. *Miles: The Autobiography.* Touchstone Press, 1989.

Davis, Sammy, Jr. *Yes I Can.* Farrar, Strauss, and Giroux, 1990.

Delaney, Sarah and A. Elizabeth with Amy Hill Hearth. *Having Our Say: The Delaney Sisters' First 100 Years.* Kodansha America, 1993.

Diggs, Anita Doreen. *Success at Work: A Guide for African-Americans.* Barricade Books, 1993.

Donadio, Stephen, Joan Smith, Susan Mesner, and Rebecca Davison. *The New York Public Library Book of 20th Century American Quotations.* Stonesong Press, 1992.

Douglass, Frederick. *Life and Times of Frederick Douglass.* Collier/Macmillan, 1962.

DuBois, W. E. B. *John Brown.* Kraus International, 1909.

DuBois, W. E. B. *The Souls of Black Folk.* Signet, 1903.

Edelman, Marian Wright. *The Measure of Our Success: A Letter to My Children and Yours.* Beacon Press, 1992.

Edwards, Audrey and Dr. Craig Polite. *Children of the Dream: The Psychology of Black Success.* Doubleday, 1992.

Ellison, Ralph. *Shadow and Act.* Random House, 1972.

Ehrlich, Scott. *Paul Robeson.* Melrose Square, 1988.

Evers, Mrs. Medgar. *For Us, the Living.* Doubleday, 1967.

Frazier, E. Franklin. *Black Bourgeoise.* Free Press/Macmillan, 1962.

Frazier, E. Franklin. *The Negro in the United States.* Macmillan, 1957.

Goggin, Jacqueline. *Carter G. Woodson.* Louisiana State University Press, 1993.

Gallen, David. *Malcolm A to X.* Carroll & Graf, 1992.

Gates, Henry Louis, Jr. *Reading Black, Reading Feminist.* Meridian, 1990.

Golden, Marita. *Wild Women Don't Wear No Blues.* Doubleday, 1993.

Gourse, Leslie. *Unforgettable: The Life and Mystique of Nat "King" Cole.* St. Martin's Press, 1991.

Haley, Alex. *The Autobiography of Malcolm X.* Grove Press, 1964.

Hansberry, Lorraine. *To Be Young, Gifted and Black.* Signet Books, 1970.

Hare, Nathan. *The Black Anglo-Saxons.* Third World Press, 1991.

Haskins, James. *Barbara Jordan.* Dial Press, 1977.

Haskins, Jim and N. R. Mitgang. *Mr. Bojangles: The Biography of Bill Robinson.* Morrow, 1988.

Hodges, Geraldyn. *Black Society.* Johnson, 1976.

Hughes, Langston. *The Big Sea.* Braziller, 1981.

Hughes, Langston. *The Book of Negro Humor.* Braziller, 1981.

Hughes, Langston. *Simple Takes a Wife.* Braziller, 1981.

Hutchinson, Earl Ofari, Ph.D. *Black Fatherhood: The Guide to Male Parenting.* Impact, 1992.

Jackson, George. *Soledad Brother: The Prison Letters of George Jackson.* Bantam, 1972.

Jackson, Reggie. *Reggie.* Ballantine, 1984.

Jefferson, Margo and Elliott P. Skinner. *Roots of Time: A Portrait of African Life and Culture.* Africa World Press, 1990.

Johnson, John H. *Succeeding Against the Odds.* Amistad, 1993.

Jones, James Earl and Penelope Niven. *Voices and Silence.* Scribner's, 1993.

Jordan, Michael. *Rare Jordan.* HarperCollins, 1993.

Katz, William Loren. *The Black West.* Doubleday, 1971.

King, Martin Luther, Jr. *Where Do We Go from Here: Chaos or Community.* Mentor, 1978.

King, Martin Luther, Jr. *Why We Can't Wait.* Mentor, 1964.

King, Norman. *Arsenio Hall.* Morrow, 1993.

Kitt, Eartha. *Confessions of a Sex Kitten.* Sidgwick & Jackson Limited, 1989.

Klein, Michael. *The Man Behind the Sound Bite.* Castillo International, 1991.

Lanker, Brian. *I Dream a World.* Stewart, Tabori & Chang, 1989.

Lerner, Gerda. *Black Women in White America.* Random House, 1992.

Lewis, David Levering. *When Harlem Was in Vogue.* Oxford University Press, 1981.

Lomax, Louis. *When the Word Is Given.* Signet, 1963.

Lynch, Hollis. *The Black Urban Condition.* Thomas Y. Crowell, 1973.

Mathabane, Mark. *Kaffir Boy in America.* Collier, 1989.

Means, Howard. *Colin Powell.* Donald I. Fine, 1992.

Meltzer, Milton. *The Black Americans: A History in Their Own Words.* Thomas Y. Crowell, 1987.

Muhammad, Elijah. *How to Eat to Live.* Muhammad's Temple of Islam No. 2, 1972.

Njeri, Itabari. *Every Good-bye Ain't Gone.* Random House, 1990.

O'Neal, Shaquille. *Shaq Attack!* Hyperion, 1993.

Oates, Stephen B. *Let the Trumpet Sound: The Life of Martin Luther King, Jr.* Plume, 1982.

Owens, Jesse. *Jesse: The Man Who Outran Hitler.* Fawcett Gold Medal, 1978.

Parks, Carole A. *Nommo: A Literary Legacy of Black Chicago.* OBAC Writers Workshop, 1987.

Pierson, William D. *Black Legacy: America's Hidden Heritage.* University of Massachusetts Press, 1993.

Plutzik, Roberta. *Lionel Richie.* Dell, 1985.

Rampersand, Arnold. *The Life of Langston Hughes.* Oxford University Press, 1986.

Reid, Inez Smith. *Together Black Women.* The Third Press, 1975.

Ross, Diana. *Secrets of a Sparrow.* Villard, 1993.

Rowan, Carl T. *Dream Makers, Dream Breakers.* Little Brown, 1993.

Schoor, Gene. *Dave Winfield: The 23 Million Dollar Man.* Stein and Day, 1982.

Shields, Cydney & Leslie C. Shields. *Work Sister Work.* Carol Publishing, 1993.

Sifford, Charlie. *Just Let Me Play.* British American Publishing, 1992.

Smith, Ronald L. *The Cosby Book.* St. Martin's Press, 1986.

Sowell, Thomas. *The Economics and Politics of Race.* Morrow, 1985.

Sowell, Thomas. *Ethnic America.* HarperCollins, 1981.

Steele, Shelby. *The Content of Our Character.* St. Martin's Press, 1990.

Strawberry, Darryl. *Darryl.* Bantam, 1992.

Swaim, Carol M. *Black Faces, White Interests.* Harvard University Press, 1993.

Taraborrelli, J. Randy. *Call Her Miss Ross.* Birch Lane Press, 1989.

Tilley, Nannie May. *The Bright-Tobacco Industry, 1860–1929.* University of North Carolina, 1948.

Turner, Tina with Kurt Loder. *I, Tina.* William Morrow, 1986.

Tutu, Naomi. *The Words of Desmond Tutu.* Newmarket Press, 1989.

Tygiel, Jules. *Baseball's Great Experiment: Jackie Robinson and His Legacy.* Vintage, 1984.

Urquhart, Brian. *Ralph Bunche: An American Life.* W. W. Norton, 1993.

Vail, John. *Mandela: Black Nationalist Leader.* Melrose Square, 1990.

Walker, Alice. *The Temple of My Familiar.* Harcourt Brace Jovanovich, 1989.

Washington, Booker T. *Up from Slavery.* Doubleday, 1900.

Weisbrot, Robert. *Freedom Bound: A History of America's Civil Rights Movement.* Plume, 1991.

Wiley, Ralph. *What Black People Should Do Now.* Ballantine/One World, 1993.

Wilson, Erlene B. *The 100 Best Colleges For African-American Students.* Plume, 1993.

Winokur, Jon. *Friendly Advice.* Plume, 1989.

Woodson, Dr. Carter G. *The Mis-Education of the Negro.* Africa World Press, 1990.

Wright, Bruce. *Black Robes, White Justice.* Carol Publishing, 1990.

Wright, Richard. *Black Boy.* Harper & Row, 1937.

PERIODICALS

Applebome, Peter. "Shaping Her Own Dream," *The New York Times,* January 20, 1994.

Bell, Bill. "How Long, Lord Till 'Amen' and 'Shalom,' " *The Daily News,* March 27, 1994.

Bernstein, Emily M. "12 Women Call for Equality in Business," *The New York Times,* February 27, 1994.

Bethune, Mary McLeod. "My Last Will and Testament," *Ebony,* August 1955.

Caldwell, Earl. "Giuliani's a Small-time Operator Playing Mayor at City Hall," *The Daily News,* January 21, 1994.

Chambers, Gordon. "Toni Braxton's Quiet Storm," *Essence,* 1994.

Clay, Cassius. "I'm a Little Special," *Sports Illustrated,* February 24, 1964.

Coleman, Chrisena, Karen Hunter-Hodge, and Denene Millner. "Black Voices Are Heard," *The Daily News,* February 27, 1994.

Collier, Aldore. "Queen Latifah Reigns On and Off TV," *Ebony,* December 1993.

Cramer, Jerome. "Turning Public Housing Over to Resident Owners," *Time,* December 12, 1988.

Crouch, Stanley. "Propaganda No Substitute for Rich Black History," *The Daily News,* March 27, 1994.

Crouch, Stanley. "Cynics Don't See America's Strength," *The Daily News,* April 10, 1994.

Curry, George E. "Thoughtful Commentary," *Emerge,* December/January 1994.

DePriest, Tomika. "Entertainers Giving Back," *Upscale,* April 1, 1994.

Dillon, Sam. "Lessons About King for a New Generation," *The New York Times,* January 17, 1994.

Dreifus, Claudia. "Joycelyn Elders," *The New York Times,* January 30, 1994.

Dwyer, Ed. "Thea Real Thing," *USA Weekend,* January 28–30, 1994.

Ebert, Alan. "Essence of Common Sense: How a Magazine Editor Turned Struggle into Triumph." *The Daily News,* January 30, 1994.

Edelhart, Courtenay. "Ella Joyce and Dan Martin," *Black Elegance,* February/March 1994.

Farrakhan, Minister Louis. "Principles of Religion," *The Final Call*, December 22, 1993.

Gates, Henry Louis. "Black Studies: Myths or Realities," *Essence*, February 1994.

Hayes, Dianne William. "The Arsenio Hall Show," *Upscale*, April 1994.

Hevesi, Dennis. "Combating a Pocket of Crime," *The New York Times*, January 4, 1994.

Hicks, Johnathan P. "Another Powell Wants to Go to Washington," *The New York Times*, February 27, 1994.

Holmes, Steven A. "Farrakhan Decries Speech for Tone, Not Content," *The New York Times*, February 4, 1994.

Hutchinson, Earl Ofari. "No Defense For The 'N' Word," *Upscale*, April 1994.

Jones, Lisa C. "Dreaming of a Black Christmas," *Ebony*, December 1993.

Kelly, Janine. "The Dancing Spirit of Judith Jamison," *Black Elegance*, February/March 1994.

Killens, John Oliver. "Explanation of the Black Psyche," *The New York Times*, June 7, 1964.

Kroll, Jack. "Jamming with Hines," *Newsweek*, June 15, 1992.

Leavy, Walter. "Baseball's $60 Million Man," *Ebony*, September 1993.

Long, Earl G. "Enjoy, It's Yours Too . . . ," *Upscale*, April 1994.

Lyons, Gene. "Laughing with Eddie," *Newsweek*, June 3, 1983.

Martin, Douglas. "The Marketing of Kwanzaa: Black American Holiday Earns Dollars, Causing Concern," *The New York Times*, December 20, 1993.

McGrath, Ellie. "For Speed and Style, Flow with the Go," *Time*, September 19, 1988.

McIver, Denise L. "Young MC: Bustin' New Grooves," *Black Beat*, October 1993.

Norment, Lynn. "Janet Jackson," *Ebony*, September 1993.

O'Brien, Maureen. "Novelist Toni Morrison Wins Nobel Prize for Literature," *Publishers Weekly*, October 11, 1993.

O'Connor, Ian. "Hoop Star Dunks on Read Dad," *The Daily News,* February 17, 1994.

Pinkney, Andrea Davis. "Winning in the Workplace," *Essence,* March 1994.

Rhoden, William C. "Jordan Leaves a Void Even He Didn't Fill," *Emerge,* December/January 1994.

Sexton, Joe. "Langston Hughes on the IRT," *The New York Times,* March 2, 1994.

Sherrill, Stephen. "Don Byron," *The New York Times Magazine,* January 16, 1994.

Steuer, Joseph. "Dream Deferred," *The Daily News,* February 27, 1994.

Steinem, Gloria. "The Verbal Karate of Florynce R. Kennedy, Esq.," *Ms.,* March 1973.

Taylor, Susan. "Our Precious Love," *Essence,* February 1994.

Taylor, Susan. "Listen to Your Life," *Essence,* March 1994.

Thigpen, David E. "Bo Knows Pain—and Dismissal," *Time,* April 1, 1991.

Wallace, Michele. "Variations on Negation and the Heresy of Black Feminist Creativity," *Heresy Publication on Art and Politics,* Issue 24, 1989.

Werner, Louise. "The Other Famous Amos," *USA Weekend,* February 25–27, 1994.

Wilkerson, Isabel. "The Surgeon General Has People Thinking," *The New York Times,* December 31, 1993.

ADDITIONAL SOURCES

"Sexagenarian Lena Horne Talks About Her Sexiness," *Jet,* May 3, 1976.

"Hit Album Brings Lou Rawls Back," *Jet,* August 26, 1976.

"Leon and Jayne Tell Why Their Good Marriage Turned Bad," *Jet,* November 26, 1981.

"Marvin Gaye: His Tragic Death and Troubled Life," *Jet,* April 26, 1984.

"Smokey Robinson's Feel for Music Made Success," *Jet*, September 24, 1984.

"Kim Fields: How She Copes with Life in Hollywood," *Jet*, July 15, 1985.

"Michael Jackson's Book Reveals Secrets of Success," *Jet*, May 16, 1988.

"Stevie Wonder Says His Message Music May Shock but His Songs Talk About Social Wrongs," *Jet*, May 30, 1988.

"Friends Speak in Tribute to World's Greatest Entertainer," *Jet*, June 4, 1990.

"Does Decision to Close Black University in Mississippi Doom State-supported Black Colleges and Universities?," *Jet*, November 30, 1992.

"Hollywood Superagent Shares His Excitement Over New Technology and What It Means For African-Americans," *Black Elegance*, Feb/March 1994.

"Chubby Checker Makes Switch to Country Music," *Jet*, January 31, 1994.

"I'm No Hitler, Farrakhan Tells Television Host," *The New York Times*, February 27, 1994.

Ø About the Author Ø

Anita Doreen Diggs is the author *of Success at Work: A Guide for African-Americans* and *The African American Resource Guide*. She lives in New York City with her husband Matthew and daughters Tayannah and Lateisha.